African Civilizations through Ages

Teadi Peter

Published by Teadi Peter, 2024.

While every precaution has been taken in the preparation of this book, the publisher assumes no responsibility for errors or omissions, or for damages resulting from the use of the information contained herein.

AFRICAN CIVILIZATIONS THROUGH AGES

First edition. May 13, 2024.

Copyright © 2024 Teadi Peter.

ISBN: 979-8224389469

Written by Teadi Peter.

Table of Contents

"The African Civilizations through Ages"

In the annals of human history, Africa stands as a continent of immense diversity, complexity, and cultural richness. From the ancient kingdoms of Egypt and Kush to the vibrant empires of Ghana, Mali, and Songhai, Africa's past is replete with stories of innovation, achievement, and resilience. Yet, despite its pivotal role in shaping the course of human civilization, the history of Africa remains too often overlooked or misunderstood. In "The African Civilizations through Ages," we embark on a journey across time and space to uncover the untold narratives of Africa's past and present.

Turning our gaze westward, we encounter the mighty empires of West Africa, where wealth, power, and prestige intersected along the trans-Saharan trade routes. From the legendary wealth of Ghana to the scholarly splendor of Timbuktu, these empires—Ghana, Mali, and Songhai—stand as testaments to the ingenuity and resilience of Africa's medieval civilizations. Through the stories of Mansa Musa, Sundiata Keita, and Askia Muhammad, we delve into the political intrigues, cultural achievements, and economic prowess of West Africa's golden age.

· · · ·

VENTURING SOUTHWARD, we explore the lesser-known realms of southern Africa, where the kingdoms of Great Zimbabwe, Mapungubwe, and the Zulu rose to prominence. Amidst the lush landscapes of the Limpopo and Zambezi rivers, these civilizations flourished, leaving behind a legacy of monumental architecture, intricate trade networks, and vibrant cultural traditions. From the stone walls of Great Zimbabwe to the golden treasures of Mapungubwe, we uncover the hidden gems of southern Africa's past.

Our journey concludes in the enigmatic lands of East Africa, where ancient port cities, such as Kilwa and Mogadishu, thrived as centers of commerce and culture. Here, amidst the shores of the Indian Ocean, we encounter the Swahili city-states, whose cosmopolitan societies embraced diverse influences from across the Indian Ocean world. From the ivory trade of Pate to the maritime exploits of the Swahili merchants, East Africa's maritime legacy unfolds before us, revealing the interconnectedness of Africa with the wider world.

Our exploration ends with the cradle of civilization itself: ancient Egypt. Here, amidst the sands of the Nile, we discover the grandeur of the pharaohs, the mysteries of the pyramids, and the enduring legacy of a civilization that flourished for millennia. From the legendary reign of King Menes to the golden age of the New Kingdom, Egypt's contributions to art, architecture, and religion reverberate through the ages, leaving an indelible mark on the world.

. . . .

AS WE REACH THE END of our odyssey through Africa's past, we are left with a profound appreciation for the continent's enduring resilience, cultural diversity, and historical significance. From the ancient civilizations of Egypt and Kush to the medieval empires of West Africa and the maritime kingdoms of East Africa, "The African Civilizations through Ages" illuminates the complexities and contradictions of Africa's past. Through its pages, we discover not only the triumphs and tribulations of Africa's civilizations but also the enduring spirit of innovation, creativity, and resilience that continues to shape the continent's destiny.

The Sultanate of Sennar, also known as the Funj Sultanate or Sennar Sultanate, was a powerful Islamic state that emerged in the region of modern-day Sudan in the 16th century. Spanning from the 1500s to the late 1800s, the Sultanate of Sennar left an indelible mark on the history and culture of the Nile Valley. From its origins to its decline, this essay will delve into the various aspects of the Sennar Sultanate, detailing its history, governance, economy, society, culture, and legacy.

Origins of the Sultanate of Sennar:

The Sultanate of Sennar traces its roots to the collapse of the Christian kingdom of Alodia in the 14th century and the subsequent influx of Arab traders and Islamic missionaries into the region. Over time, a series of indigenous African kingdoms, such as the Funj and the Keira, emerged in the fertile plains of the Blue Nile, laying the foundation for the future sultanate. The consolidation of power under the Funj dynasty in the 15th century marked the beginning of the Sennar Sultanate's rise to prominence.

• • • •

GOVERNANCE AND ADMINISTRATION:

At its zenith, the Sultanate of Sennar was governed by a complex system of centralized authority and provincial administration. The sultan, who ruled from the capital city of Sennar, held absolute power and was considered both a political and religious leader. Beneath the sultan were appointed governors, known as emirs, who oversaw the administration of various provinces and cities. Local governance was further facilitated by a network of tribal chiefs and religious leaders who helped maintain order and stability throughout the realm.

• • • •

ECONOMY AND TRADE:

The economy of the Sultanate of Sennar was largely agrarian, relying on the fertile lands of the Nile Valley for the cultivation of crops such as wheat, barley, sorghum, and millet. The kingdom's strategic location along the trade routes linking East Africa to the Mediterranean facilitated the exchange of goods such as ivory, gold, slaves, and exotic spices. Sennar's control over key trade routes allowed it to amass considerable wealth and exert influence over neighboring states.

Society and Culture:

Sennar was a diverse and cosmopolitan society, home to people of various ethnicities, languages, and religious beliefs. While Islam served as the dominant faith, coexisting with traditional African religions, the sultanate was known for its religious tolerance and pluralism. Arabic served as the lingua franca of the elite, while indigenous languages such as Nubian and Beja were spoken by the majority of the population. The arts flourished under Sennar's patronage, with poets, musicians, and calligraphers producing works of great beauty and sophistication.

• • • •

MILITARY AND DEFENSE:

The military played a crucial role in the expansion and defense of the Sultanate of Sennar. The sultanate maintained a standing army composed of professional soldiers, supplemented by tribal levies and mercenaries drawn from neighboring regions. Cavalry, armed with spears, swords, and bows, formed the backbone of Sennar's military forces, while infantry and artillery provided support on the battlefield. Sennar's military prowess allowed it to fend off incursions from rival states and exert control over vast territories.

Decline and Legacy:

Despite its formidable strength, the Sultanate of Sennar began to decline in the late 18th century due to internal strife, external pressures, and the encroachment of European colonial powers. The kingdom's fragmentation into rival factions weakened its ability to resist outside aggression, culminating in its eventual conquest by the forces of Muhammad Ali of Egypt in the early 19th century. Though the Sultanate of Sennar ceased to exist as a political entity, its legacy endured in the collective memory of the Sudanese people, serving as a symbol of resilience, cultural diversity, and historical continuity.

The Sultanate of Sennar stands as a testament to the complexities of African history and the enduring legacies of Islamic civilization. From its humble origins to its eventual demise, Sennar's story is one of conquest and consolidation, of prosperity and decline. Through its governance, economy, society, culture, military, and legacy, the Sultanate of Sennar left an indelible mark on the history of the Nile Valley and the broader Islamic world.

Kingdom of Kush

The Kingdom of Kush, also known as the Kingdom of Napata or the Kingdom of Meroë, was an ancient African civilization that flourished along the Nile River in what is now Sudan. From its origins in the Bronze Age to its eventual decline in the 4th century AD, the Kingdom of Kush left an indelible mark on the history and culture of northeastern Africa. In this essay, we will explore the rich history, culture, economy, society, religion, architecture, and legacy of the Kingdom of Kush.

• • • •

ORIGINS AND EARLY HISTORY:

The Kingdom of Kush emerged around 2000 BC in the region known as Nubia, situated between the first and sixth cataracts of the Nile River. Initially a collection of small, independent villages, Kush gradually coalesced into a centralized state with its capital at Kerma. The kingdom's strategic location along the Nile facilitated trade and cultural exchange with neighboring civilizations, including ancient Egypt.

Rise to Power:

Kush's fortunes changed dramatically during the New Kingdom period of ancient Egypt (16th to 11th centuries BC), when it became a major power in the region. The conquests of Egyptian pharaohs such as Thutmose III and Amenhotep II extended Egyptian influence into Nubia, leading to the establishment of Egyptian administrative centers and garrisons in the region. However, rather than being subjugated, the Kingdom of Kush eventually emerged as a formidable rival to Egypt, culminating in the expulsion of Egyptian forces from Nubia around 1070 BC.

• • • •

CAPITAL AT NAPATA:

Following the expulsion of the Egyptians, the Kingdom of Kush entered a period of expansion and prosperity. The capital was moved from Kerma to Napata, located further south along the Nile. Napata became a thriving urban center, boasting impressive architecture, monumental temples, and royal palaces. The kingdom's rulers, known as the "Black Pharaohs," adopted many aspects of Egyptian culture and religion while retaining their own distinct identity.

Economy and Trade:

The economy of the Kingdom of Kush was based primarily on agriculture, with the cultivation of crops such as wheat, barley, millet, and sorghum supporting a growing population. The kingdom's access to the Nile River facilitated irrigation and provided fertile soil for farming. Additionally, Kush controlled important trade routes linking sub-Saharan Africa with the Mediterranean world, enabling the exchange of goods such as gold, ivory, incense, and exotic animals.

• • • •

SOCIETY AND CULTURE:

Kushite society was hierarchical, with a ruling class of nobles and priests overseeing the administration of the kingdom. Below them were artisans, merchants, and farmers, while slaves performed menial labor. The Kushites were skilled craftsmen, renowned for their pottery, jewelry, textiles, and metalwork. They also excelled in the production of monumental architecture, with temples, pyramids, and palaces dotting the landscape of Napata and Meroë.

Religion and Beliefs:

Religion played a central role in Kushite life, with the worship of a pantheon of gods and goddesses similar to those of ancient Egypt. The most important deity was Amun, the god of the sun and kingship, who was venerated as the patron deity of the Kushite rulers. Other important gods included Anukis, the goddess of the Nile, and Apedemak, the lion-headed god of war. Temples dedicated to these deities served as centers of religious and political power.

· · · ·

DECLINE AND LEGACY:

The Kingdom of Kush reached its zenith during the Meroitic period (4th century BC to 4th century AD), when it controlled vast territories stretching from the Nile Delta to the Blue Nile. However, internal strife, external pressures, and the decline of trade routes contributed to the kingdom's gradual decline. The rise of the Kingdom of Axum in neighboring Ethiopia further weakened Kush's position, eventually leading to its conquest by the Axumites in the 4th century AD.

Despite its eventual demise, the Kingdom of Kush left a lasting legacy that endures to this day. Its rich cultural heritage, architectural achievements, and contributions to world civilization continue to fascinate scholars and enthusiasts alike. From its humble origins as a collection of small villages to its status as a regional powerhouse, the Kingdom of Kush stands as a testament to the resilience, ingenuity, and enduring spirit of ancient African civilization.

The Kingdom of Aksum, also spelled Axum, was an ancient civilization located in the Horn of Africa, in what is now Ethiopia and Eritrea. Flourishing from around the 1st century AD to the 7th century AD, the Kingdom of Aksum was a major player in regional and international trade, a center of early Christianity, and known for its monumental architecture and cultural achievements. In this essay, we will explore the history, culture, economy, society, religion, architecture, and legacy of the Kingdom of Aksum.

• • • •

ORIGINS AND EARLY HISTORY:

The Kingdom of Aksum emerged in the northern Ethiopian highlands around the 1st century AD, likely as a result of the amalgamation of indigenous Cushitic-speaking peoples with immigrants from the Arabian Peninsula. The region's strategic location at the crossroads of trade routes linking the Red Sea with the interior of Africa and the Arabian Peninsula facilitated the kingdom's rapid growth and prosperity.

• • • •

RISE TO POWER:

Aksum's rise to prominence was closely linked to its control over trade routes, particularly the Red Sea trade route, which connected the kingdom with the Roman Empire, India, and the Arabian Peninsula. Aksum became a major hub for the exchange of goods such as ivory, gold, frankincense, and spices, accruing considerable wealth and influence in the process. The kingdom's rulers, known as neguses (kings), expanded their territory through conquest and diplomacy, establishing a vast maritime empire that extended as far as modern-day Yemen and Saudi Arabia.

. . . .

CAPITAL AT AKSUM:

The capital of the Kingdom of Aksum was the city of Aksum, located in present-day northern Ethiopia. Aksum served as the political, economic, and cultural center of the kingdom, boasting impressive architecture, monumental obelisks, and royal palaces. The city's most iconic landmark, the Aksum Obelisks, stood as symbols of the kingdom's power and prosperity, with some reaching heights of over 20 meters.

. . . .

ECONOMY AND TRADE:

The economy of the Kingdom of Aksum was primarily based on trade, with the kingdom's access to the Red Sea enabling it to dominate regional commerce. Aksumite merchants traded goods such as ivory, gold, slaves, spices, and exotic animals with merchants from the Roman Empire, Persia, India, and beyond. Aksum's control over trade routes allowed it to accumulate vast wealth, which was reflected in the kingdom's impressive architecture, sophisticated urban centers, and luxurious lifestyle of its elite.

. . . .

SOCIETY AND CULTURE:

Aksumite society was hierarchical, with a ruling class of nobles and priests overseeing the administration of the kingdom. Below them were merchants, artisans, farmers, and laborers, while slaves performed menial tasks. The Aksumites were skilled craftsmen, known for their pottery, metalwork, and intricate carvings. They also excelled in the production of monumental architecture, with palaces, temples, and stelae serving as symbols of royal power and religious devotion.

· · · ·

RELIGION AND CHRISTIANITY:

The religion of the Kingdom of Aksum was a blend of indigenous animistic beliefs and influences from Judaism, Christianity, and later, Islam. The Aksumites worshiped a pantheon of gods and goddesses, including Mahrem, the god of war, and Astar, the goddess of fertility. However, the most significant religious development in Aksum was the adoption of Christianity in the 4th century AD, making it one of the earliest Christian kingdoms in the world. The conversion of King Ezana to Christianity and the establishment of the Ethiopian Orthodox Tewahedo Church as the kingdom's official religion marked a significant turning point in Aksumite history.

Decline and Legacy:

The decline of the Kingdom of Aksum began in the 7th century AD, with the rise of Islam and the decline of trade routes linking the Red Sea with the Mediterranean world. The kingdom's maritime empire was gradually eroded by Arab invaders, while internal conflicts and environmental factors further weakened Aksum's position. By the 10th century AD, Aksum had been reduced to a regional power, overshadowed by the emerging Ethiopian kingdoms of the highlands.

Despite its decline, the Kingdom of Aksum left a lasting legacy that continues to shape the cultural identity of modern Ethiopia and Eritrea. Its architectural achievements, including the Aksum Obelisks and the ruins of Aksumite palaces and temples, are UNESCO World Heritage Sites that attract tourists and scholars from around the world. Additionally, the adoption of Christianity by the Aksumite rulers laid the foundation for the Ethiopian Orthodox Church, which remains a vibrant and influential religious institution to this day. Overall, the

Kingdom of Aksum stands as a testament to the ingenuity, resilience, and enduring legacy of one of Africa's most influential civilizations.

Ghana Empire

The Ghana Empire, also known as the Wagadou Empire, was one of the most influential civilizations in West Africa during the medieval period. Flourishing from approximately the 6th to the 13th century AD, the Ghana Empire was renowned for its wealth, power, and control over trans-Saharan trade routes. In this essay, we will explore the history, economy, society, culture, governance, religion, and legacy of the Ghana Empire.

. . . .

ORIGINS AND EARLY HISTORY:

The origins of the Ghana Empire can be traced back to the Soninke people, who inhabited the region of modern-day southeastern Mauritania and western Mali. The kingdom of Ghana emerged around the 6th century AD, consolidating smaller chiefdoms and tribes under a centralized authority. The capital of the Ghana Empire was Kumbi Saleh, a bustling urban center that served as a hub for trade and administration.

Economy and Trans-Saharan Trade:

The economy of the Ghana Empire was based primarily on agriculture, with the cultivation of crops such as millet, sorghum, and rice supporting a growing population. However, the empire's true source of wealth lay in its control over trans-Saharan trade routes. Ghana's strategic location between the gold-rich regions of West Africa and the Mediterranean world allowed it to monopolize the trade in gold, salt, ivory, and slaves. Caravans of camel-mounted traders, known as the "Saharan caravaneers," traversed the desert, exchanging goods with merchants from North Africa and the Middle East.

• • • •

SOCIETY AND CULTURE:

Ghanaian society was hierarchical, with a ruling class of nobles and elites overseeing the administration of the empire. Below them were merchants, artisans, farmers, and laborers, while slaves performed menial tasks. The Ghanaian people were skilled craftsmen, known for their pottery, weaving, metalwork, and leatherworking. They also excelled in the production of elaborate jewelry and textiles, which were highly prized commodities in the trans-Saharan trade network.

Governance and Administration:

The Ghana Empire was governed by a centralized monarchy, with power concentrated in the hands of the king, or "Ghana." The Ghana ruled from Kumbi Saleh and exercised authority over a network of provincial governors, known as "kings of the land." Local governance was facilitated by a system of tributary states and client kingdoms, which paid homage to the Ghana in exchange for protection and trade privileges. The empire's legal system was based on customary law and Islamic jurisprudence, with judges and councils presiding over disputes and grievances.

• • • •

RELIGION AND ISLAMIZATION:

The religion of the Ghana Empire was a blend of indigenous animistic beliefs and Islamic influences. While the majority of the population adhered to traditional African religions, Islam gained a foothold in Ghana through trade contacts with Muslim merchants from North Africa and the Middle East. Over time, Islam became increasingly influential in Ghanaian society, with the adoption of Arabic script, Islamic legal practices, and the construction of mosques in major cities such as Kumbi Saleh.

Decline and Legacy:

The decline of the Ghana Empire began in the 11th century AD, as external pressures, internal conflicts, and the rise of rival states weakened its position. The Almoravid invasion in the 11th century dealt a severe blow to Ghana's control over trans-Saharan trade routes, while the emergence of new trading centers such as Mali and Songhai further eroded its influence. By the 13th century AD, Ghana had been reduced to a shadow of its former glory, eventually succumbing to conquest by the Mali Empire.

Despite its decline, the Ghana Empire left a lasting legacy that continues to shape the cultural identity of modern West Africa. Its role as a commercial and cultural crossroads facilitated the exchange of ideas, languages, and technologies across the Sahara Desert. The legacy of the Ghana Empire lives on in the oral traditions, folklore, and historical memory of the region, serving as a symbol of West Africa's rich and diverse heritage.

The Songhai Empire, also spelled Songhay or Songhai, was one of the most powerful and influential empires in West Africa during the 15th and 16th centuries. Emerging from the remnants of the Mali Empire, the Songhai Empire reached its zenith under the leadership of Sunni Ali and Askia Muhammad I. Known for its military prowess, administrative efficiency, and cultural achievements, the Songhai Empire left an indelible mark on the history and culture of the Sahel region. In this essay, we will explore the history, economy, society, culture, governance, religion, and legacy of the Songhai Empire.

. . . .

ORIGINS AND EARLY HISTORY:

The origins of the Songhai Empire can be traced back to the collapse of the Mali Empire in the late 14th century. In the aftermath of Mali's decline, a series of small kingdoms and city-states emerged in the region of modern-day Mali, Niger, and Burkina Faso. One of these kingdoms was Songhai, located along the Niger River in the western Sahel. Over time, Songhai expanded its territory through conquest and diplomacy, laying the foundation for the emergence of a unified empire.

. . . .

RISE TO POWER:

The rise of the Songhai Empire can be attributed to the military conquests of Sunni Ali, who seized power in the late 15th century and embarked on a campaign of expansion and consolidation. Sunni Ali's forces defeated rival kingdoms such as the Mali Empire, the Mossi Kingdoms, and the Hausa city-states, establishing Songhai as the dominant power in the region. Under Sunni Ali's leadership, Songhai reached its territorial peak, stretching from the Atlantic coast in the west to the Lake Chad basin in the east.

. . . .

ECONOMY AND TRADE:

The economy of the Songhai Empire was based primarily on agriculture, with the cultivation of crops such as millet, sorghum, rice, and cotton supporting a growing population. However, trade also played a significant role in the empire's economy, with Songhai controlling key trade routes linking West Africa with North Africa and the Mediterranean world. The empire's strategic location along the Niger River facilitated the exchange of goods such as gold, salt, ivory, slaves, and textiles.

. . . .

SOCIETY AND CULTURE:

Songhai society was hierarchical, with a ruling class of nobles, bureaucrats, and military officers overseeing the administration of the empire. Below them were merchants, artisans, farmers, and laborers, while slaves performed menial tasks. The Songhai people were known for their skill in metallurgy, pottery, weaving, and leatherworking, producing intricate and finely crafted goods that were highly prized in the regional trade networks. Additionally, Songhai culture flourished under the patronage of the empire's rulers, with poets, musicians, and scholars producing works of great beauty and sophistication.

. . . .

GOVERNANCE AND ADMINISTRATION:

The Songhai Empire was governed by a centralized monarchy, with power concentrated in the hands of the emperor, or "Askia." The empire was divided into administrative provinces, each overseen by a governor appointed by the emperor. Local governance was facilitated by a system of tributary states and client kingdoms, which paid homage to the emperor in exchange for protection and trade privileges. The empire's legal system was based on Islamic law, with judges and qadis presiding over disputes and grievances.

. . . .

RELIGION AND ISLAMIZATION:

The religion of the Songhai Empire was a blend of indigenous animistic beliefs and Islamic influences. Islam gained a foothold in Songhai through trade contacts with Muslim merchants from North Africa and the Middle East, as well as through the efforts of Islamic missionaries and scholars. Over time, Islam became increasingly influential in Songhai society, with the adoption of Arabic script, Islamic legal practices, and the construction of mosques in major cities such as Gao and Timbuktu.

. . . .

DECLINE AND LEGACY:

The decline of the Songhai Empire began in the late 16th century, as internal strife, external pressures, and the rise of rival states weakened its position. The empire's vulnerability was exploited by Moroccan invaders, who launched a series of military campaigns against Songhai in the early 17th century. Despite fierce resistance, the Songhai forces were ultimately defeated, and the empire collapsed under the weight of Moroccan conquest.

Despite its eventual demise, the Songhai Empire left a lasting legacy that continues to shape the culture and history of West Africa. Its military achievements, administrative innovations, and cultural contributions laid the foundation for subsequent states and empires in the region. The legacy of the Songhai Empire lives on in the oral traditions, folklore, and historical memory of the region, serving as a symbol of West Africa's rich and diverse heritage.

The Kingdom of Meroë, also spelled Meroe, was an ancient civilization located in the Nile Valley region of present-day Sudan. Flourishing from approximately 800 BC to 350 AD, the Kingdom of Meroë was a significant center of power and culture in northeastern Africa. In this essay, we will explore the history, economy, society, culture, governance, religion, architecture, and legacy of the Kingdom of Meroë.

Origins and Early History:

The origins of the Kingdom of Meroë can be traced back to the decline of the Kingdom of Kush around the 8th century BC. As Kushite power waned, a new dynasty of rulers emerged in the city of Meroë, located along the Nile River in what is now northern Sudan. These rulers, known as the "Candaces" or "Kandakes," established Meroë as the capital of a new kingdom that would come to dominate the region for centuries.

Rise to Power:

The Kingdom of Meroë reached its zenith during the Meroitic period (4th century BC to 4th century AD), when it controlled vast territories stretching from the Nile Delta to the Blue Nile. Meroë's strategic location along the Nile facilitated trade and cultural exchange with neighboring civilizations, including Egypt, Nubia, and the Red Sea coast. The kingdom's rulers, known for their military prowess and diplomatic skill, expanded Meroë's influence through conquest and alliance-building, establishing a network of tributary states and client kingdoms.

· · · ·

ECONOMY AND TRADE:

The economy of the Kingdom of Meroë was based primarily on agriculture, with the cultivation of crops such as sorghum, millet, barley, and wheat supporting a growing population. Meroë's access to the Nile River facilitated irrigation and provided fertile soil for farming. Additionally, the kingdom controlled important trade routes linking sub-Saharan Africa with the Mediterranean world, enabling the exchange of goods such as ivory, gold, incense, and exotic animals.

• • • •

SOCIETY AND CULTURE:

Meroitic society was hierarchical, with a ruling class of nobles, priests, and bureaucrats overseeing the administration of the kingdom. Below them were artisans, merchants, farmers, and laborers, while slaves performed menial tasks. The Meroitic people were skilled craftsmen, known for their pottery, jewelry, textiles, and metalwork. They also excelled in the production of monumental architecture, with temples, pyramids, and palaces serving as symbols of royal power and religious devotion.

• • • •

GOVERNANCE AND ADMINISTRATION:

The Kingdom of Meroë was governed by a centralized monarchy, with power concentrated in the hands of the Candace, or queen. The Candace ruled from the royal capital of Meroë and exercised authority over a network of provincial governors, known as "kings of the land." Local governance was facilitated by a system of tributary states and client kingdoms, which paid homage to the Candace in exchange for protection and trade privileges. The kingdom's legal system was based on customary law and Meroitic traditions, with judges and councils presiding over disputes and grievances.

• • • •

RELIGION AND BELIEFS:

Religion played a central role in Meroitic life, with the worship of a pantheon of gods and goddesses similar to those of ancient Egypt. The most important deity was Amun, the god of the sun and kingship, who was venerated as the patron deity of the Meroitic rulers. Other important gods included Isis, Osiris, Horus, and Anubis, whose cults flourished in Meroë's temples and sanctuaries. The Meroitic religion also included elements of indigenous African beliefs, such as ancestor worship and nature reverence.

Decline and Legacy:

The decline of the Kingdom of Meroë began in the 4th century AD, as external pressures, internal conflicts, and the decline of trade routes weakened its position. The kingdom's vulnerability was exploited by neighboring powers, including the Kingdom of Aksum and the Roman Empire, who launched military campaigns against Meroë in the late antiquity period. By the 4th century AD, Meroë had been reduced to a shadow of its former glory, eventually succumbing to conquest and assimilation by the emerging Christian kingdoms of Nubia.

Despite its decline, the Kingdom of Meroë left a lasting legacy that continues to shape the culture and history of Sudan and the broader Nile Valley region. Its monumental architecture, sophisticated urban centers, and cultural achievements are a testament to the ingenuity, resilience, and enduring spirit of one of Africa's most remarkable civilizations. The legacy of the Kingdom of Meroë lives on in the archaeological sites, artifacts, and oral traditions of Sudan, serving as a source of inspiration and pride for generations to come.

Nubian Kingdom of Alodia

The Nubian Kingdom of Alodia, also known as Alwa or Alwa Kingdom, was a medieval African civilization located in the region of present-day Sudan. Flourishing from approximately the 6th to the 14th century AD, the Kingdom of Alodia was a powerful and culturally rich state that played a significant role in the history of northeastern Africa. In this essay, we will explore the history, economy, society, culture, governance, religion, architecture, and legacy of the Nubian Kingdom of Alodia.

• • • •

ORIGINS AND EARLY HISTORY:

The Kingdom of Alodia traces its origins to the collapse of the Kingdom of Kush in the 4th century AD. Following the decline of Kushite power, a new dynasty of rulers emerged in the region of Alodia, situated between the Nile and Atbara rivers in what is now northern Sudan. The Alodian kings, known as the "Makkurians," established Alodia as a center of power and culture, inheriting the legacy of Kushite civilization while forging their own distinct identity.

Rise to Power:

The Kingdom of Alodia reached its zenith during the medieval period, when it became a major player in regional politics and trade. Under the leadership of kings such as Merkurios and Zacharias, Alodia expanded its territory through conquest and alliance-building, establishing a network of tributary states and client kingdoms. Alodia's strategic location along the Nile facilitated trade and cultural exchange with neighboring civilizations, including Egypt, Nubia, and the Red Sea coast.

• • • •

ECONOMY AND TRADE:

The economy of the Kingdom of Alodia was based primarily on agriculture, with the cultivation of crops such as wheat, barley, millet, and sorghum supporting a growing population. Alodia's access to the Nile and Atbara rivers facilitated irrigation and provided fertile soil for farming. Additionally, the kingdom controlled important trade routes linking sub-Saharan Africa with the Mediterranean world, enabling the exchange of goods such as ivory, gold, incense, and exotic animals.

• • • •

SOCIETY AND CULTURE:

Alodian society was hierarchical, with a ruling class of nobles, priests, and bureaucrats overseeing the administration of the kingdom. Below them were artisans, merchants, farmers, and laborers, while slaves performed menial tasks. The Alodian people were skilled craftsmen, known for their pottery, jewelry, textiles, and metalwork. They also excelled in the production of monumental architecture, with temples, palaces, and fortifications serving as symbols of royal power and religious devotion.

• • • •

GOVERNANCE AND ADMINISTRATION:

The Kingdom of Alodia was governed by a centralized monarchy, with power concentrated in the hands of the king, or "Makkuria." The Makkuria ruled from the royal capital of Soba and exercised authority over a network of provincial governors, known as "kings of the land." Local governance was facilitated by a system of tributary states and client kingdoms, which paid homage to the Makkuria in exchange for protection and trade privileges. The kingdom's legal system was based on customary law and Alodian traditions, with judges and councils presiding over disputes and grievances.

• • • •

RELIGION AND BELIEFS:

Religion played a central role in Alodian life, with the worship of a pantheon of gods and goddesses similar to those of ancient Egypt and Nubia. The most important deity was Apedemak, the lion-headed god of war and kingship, who was venerated as the patron deity of the Alodian rulers. Other important gods included Amun, Osiris, Isis, and Horus, whose cults flourished in Alodia's temples and sanctuaries. The Alodian religion also included elements of indigenous African beliefs, such as ancestor worship and nature reverence.

Decline and Legacy:

The decline of the Kingdom of Alodia began in the 14th century AD, as external pressures, internal conflicts, and the decline of trade routes weakened its position. The kingdom's vulnerability was exploited by neighboring powers, including the Sultanate of Funj and the emerging Christian kingdoms of Ethiopia, who launched military campaigns against Alodia in the late medieval period. By the 15th century AD, Alodia had been reduced to a shadow of its former glory, eventually succumbing to conquest and assimilation by the Funj Sultanate.

Despite its decline, the Kingdom of Alodia left a lasting legacy that continues to shape the culture and history of Sudan and the broader Nile Valley region. Its monumental architecture, sophisticated urban centers, and cultural achievements are a testament to the ingenuity, resilience, and enduring spirit of one of Africa's most remarkable civilizations. The legacy of the Kingdom of Alodia lives on in the archaeological sites, artifacts, and oral traditions of Sudan, serving as a source of inspiration and pride for generations to come.

Nubian Kingdom of Makuria

The Nubian Kingdom of Makuria was a medieval African civilization located in the region of present-day Sudan. Flourishing from approximately the 4th to the 14th century AD, the Kingdom of Makuria was a powerful and culturally rich state that played a significant role in the history of northeastern Africa. In this essay, we will explore the history, economy, society, culture, governance, religion, architecture, and legacy of the Nubian Kingdom of Makuria.

. . . .

ORIGINS AND EARLY HISTORY:

The Kingdom of Makuria emerged as a successor state to the Kingdom of Kush in the 4th century AD, following the decline of Kushite power. Located in the region of Lower Nubia, along the Nile River, Makuria inherited the legacy of Kushite civilization while forging its own distinct identity. The early rulers of Makuria, known as the "Makurians," established their capital at Dongola and gradually expanded their territory through conquest and alliance-building.

. . . .

RISE TO POWER:

Makuria reached its zenith during the medieval period, when it became a major player in regional politics and trade. Under the leadership of kings such as Merkurios and Zacharias, Makuria expanded its territory southward into Upper Nubia and northward into Lower Egypt, establishing a network of tributary states and client kingdoms. Makuria's strategic location along the Nile facilitated trade and cultural exchange with neighboring civilizations, including Egypt, Nubia, and the Red Sea coast.

ECONOMY AND TRADE:

The economy of the Kingdom of Makuria was based primarily on agriculture, with the cultivation of crops such as wheat, barley, millet, and sorghum supporting a growing population. Makuria's access to the Nile facilitated irrigation and provided fertile soil for farming. Additionally, the kingdom controlled important trade routes linking sub-Saharan Africa with the Mediterranean world, enabling the exchange of goods such as ivory, gold, incense, and exotic animals.

• • • •

SOCIETY AND CULTURE:

Makurian society was hierarchical, with a ruling class of nobles, priests, and bureaucrats overseeing the administration of the kingdom. Below them were artisans, merchants, farmers, and laborers, while slaves performed menial tasks. The Makurian people were skilled craftsmen, known for their pottery, jewelry, textiles, and metalwork. They also excelled in the production of monumental architecture, with temples, palaces, and fortifications serving as symbols of royal power and religious devotion.

• • • •

GOVERNANCE AND ADMINISTRATION:

The Kingdom of Makuria was governed by a centralized monarchy, with power concentrated in the hands of the king, or "Makurian." The Makurian ruled from the royal capital of Dongola and exercised authority over a network of provincial governors, known as "kings of the land." Local governance was facilitated by a system of tributary states and client kingdoms, which paid homage to the Makurian in exchange for protection and trade privileges. The kingdom's legal system was based on customary law and Makurian traditions, with judges and councils presiding over disputes and grievances.

• • • •

RELIGION AND BELIEFS:

Religion played a central role in Makurian life, with the worship of a pantheon of gods and goddesses similar to those of ancient Egypt and Nubia. The most important deity was Apedemak, the lion-headed god of war and kingship, who was venerated as the patron deity of the Makurian rulers. Other important gods included Amun, Osiris, Isis, and Horus, whose cults flourished in Makuria's temples and sanctuaries. The Makurian religion also included elements of indigenous African beliefs, such as ancestor worship and nature reverence.

Decline and Legacy:

The decline of the Kingdom of Makuria began in the 14th century AD, as external pressures, internal conflicts, and the decline of trade routes weakened its position. The kingdom's vulnerability was exploited by neighboring powers, including the Sultanate of Funj and the emerging Christian kingdoms of Ethiopia, who launched military campaigns against Makuria in the late medieval period. By the 15th century AD, Makuria had been reduced to a shadow of its former glory, eventually succumbing to conquest and assimilation by the Funj Sultanate.

Despite its decline, the Kingdom of Makuria left a lasting legacy that continues to shape the culture and history of Sudan and the broader Nile Valley region. Its monumental architecture, sophisticated urban centers, and cultural achievements are a testament to the ingenuity, resilience, and enduring spirit of one of Africa's most remarkable civilizations. The legacy of the Kingdom of Makuria lives on in the archaeological sites, artifacts, and oral traditions of Sudan, serving as a source of inspiration and pride for generations to come.

The Kingdom of Dʿmt, also known as Damot or Daʾamot, was an ancient civilization located in present-day Eritrea and northern Ethiopia. Flourishing from around the 10th century BC to the 5th century AD, Dʿmt was one of the earliest known states in the Horn of Africa and played a significant role in the region's history. In this essay, we will explore the history, economy, society, culture, governance, religion, architecture, and legacy of the Kingdom of Dʿmt.

• • • •

ORIGINS AND EARLY HISTORY:

The origins of the Kingdom of Dʿmt can be traced back to the migration of Semitic-speaking peoples into the Horn of Africa around the 10th century BC. These migrants, believed to have come from the Arabian Peninsula, settled in the region and established a network of city-states and trading centers. Over time, these city-states coalesced into the Kingdom of Dʿmt, with its capital likely located at Yeha or nearby areas in modern-day Eritrea.

• • • •

RISE TO POWER:

Dʿmt reached its zenith during the first millennium BC when it became a major player in regional politics and trade. The kingdom's strategic location along the Red Sea coast facilitated trade and cultural exchange with neighboring civilizations, including Egypt, Arabia, and the Levant. Dʿmt controlled important trade routes linking the interior of Africa with the Mediterranean world, enabling the exchange of goods such as ivory, gold, frankincense, and spices.

• • • •

ECONOMY AND TRADE:

The economy of the Kingdom of D'mt was based primarily on agriculture, with the cultivation of crops such as barley, wheat, teff, and millet supporting a growing population. D'mt's access to fertile soil and reliable rainfall in the highlands of Eritrea and northern Ethiopia facilitated agriculture and allowed for the development of urban centers and settlements. Additionally, the kingdom's control over trade routes enabled it to accumulate wealth through commerce and exchange.

• • • •

SOCIETY AND CULTURE:

D'mt society was hierarchical, with a ruling class of nobles, priests, and bureaucrats overseeing the administration of the kingdom. Below them were artisans, merchants, farmers, and laborers, while slaves performed menial tasks. The D'mt people were skilled craftsmen, known for their pottery, jewelry, textiles, and metalwork. They also excelled in the production of monumental architecture, with temples, palaces, and fortifications serving as symbols of royal power and religious devotion.

• • • •

GOVERNANCE AND ADMINISTRATION:

The Kingdom of D'mt was governed by a centralized monarchy, with power concentrated in the hands of the king, or "D'mti." The D'mti ruled from the royal capital and exercised authority over a network of provincial governors, known as "kings of the land." Local governance was facilitated by a system of tributary states and client kingdoms, which paid homage to the D'mti in exchange for protection and trade privileges. The kingdom's legal system was based on customary law and D'mti traditions, with judges and councils presiding over disputes and grievances.

· · · ·

RELIGION AND BELIEFS:

Religion played a central role in Dʿmti life, with the worship of a pantheon of gods and goddesses similar to those of ancient Egypt and Mesopotamia. The most important deity was Astar, the goddess of fertility and war, who was venerated as the patron deity of the Dʿmti rulers. Other important gods included Mahrem, the god of war, and Almaqah, the god of the moon and agriculture. The Dʿmti religion also included elements of indigenous African beliefs, such as ancestor worship and nature reverence.

Decline and Legacy:

The decline of the Kingdom of Dʿmt began in the 5th century AD, as external pressures, internal conflicts, and the rise of rival states weakened its position. The kingdom's vulnerability was exploited by neighboring powers, including the Aksumite Empire and the emerging Christian kingdoms of Ethiopia, who launched military campaigns against Dʿmt in the late antiquity period. By the 6th century AD, Dʿmt had been reduced to a shadow of its former glory, eventually succumbing to conquest and assimilation by the Aksumites.

Despite its decline, the Kingdom of Dʿmt left a lasting legacy that continues to shape the culture and history of Eritrea and Ethiopia. Its monumental architecture, sophisticated urban centers, and cultural achievements are a testament to the ingenuity, resilience, and enduring spirit of one of Africa's earliest civilizations. The legacy of the Kingdom of Dʿmt lives on in the archaeological sites, artifacts, and oral traditions of the region, serving as a source of inspiration and pride for generations to come.

Kingdom of Mauretania

The Kingdom of Mauretania was an ancient civilization located in the Maghreb region of North Africa, encompassing parts of modern-day Morocco, Algeria, and Mauritania. Flourishing from approximately the 3rd century BC to the 5th century AD, Mauretania was a significant political and cultural power in the ancient world. In this essay, we will explore the history, economy, society, culture, governance, religion, architecture, and legacy of the Kingdom of Mauretania.

. . . .

ORIGINS AND EARLY HISTORY:

The Kingdom of Mauretania traces its origins to the Berber tribes that inhabited the region of ancient Numidia and Mauritania. The kingdom emerged as a political entity during the 3rd century BC, when the Berber chieftain Baga established his rule over the region. Over time, Mauretania expanded its territory through conquest and alliance-building, establishing a network of urban centers, fortifications, and trade routes.

. . . .

RISE TO POWER:

Mauretania reached its zenith during the reign of King Juba II in the 1st century BC and 1st century AD. Juba II, a Roman client king, embarked on a program of urban development, cultural exchange, and economic reform that transformed Mauretania into a prosperous and cosmopolitan kingdom. Under Juba II's rule, Mauretania became a major center of trade and commerce, linking the Mediterranean world with sub-Saharan Africa and the Atlantic coast.

ECONOMY AND TRADE:

The economy of the Kingdom of Mauretania was based primarily on agriculture, with the cultivation of crops such as wheat, barley, olives, and grapes supporting a growing population. Mauretania's access to fertile soil and abundant water sources facilitated agriculture and allowed for the development of urban centers and settlements. Additionally, the kingdom controlled important trade routes linking North Africa with Europe, the Middle East, and sub-Saharan Africa, enabling the exchange of goods such as grain, olive oil, wine, pottery, and textiles.

• • • •

SOCIETY AND CULTURE:

Mauretanian society was diverse and multicultural, with Berber, Roman, and Punic influences shaping its identity. The kingdom was home to a diverse population of Berbers, Romans, Phoenicians, Greeks, and Jews, who coexisted and intermingled in urban centers such as Tingis (modern-day Tangier) and Volubilis. Mauretanian culture was characterized by its rich traditions of art, literature, music, and cuisine, as well as its tolerance and openness to foreign influences.

• • • •

GOVERNANCE AND ADMINISTRATION:

The Kingdom of Mauretania was governed by a centralized monarchy, with power concentrated in the hands of the king, or "Mauretanian." The Mauretanian ruled from the royal capital of Iol, overseeing a network of provincial governors, military commanders, and local administrators. Local governance was facilitated by a system of tributary states and client kingdoms, which paid homage to the Mauretanian in exchange for protection and trade privileges. The kingdom's legal system was based on customary law and Roman jurisprudence, with judges and councils presiding over disputes and grievances.

• • • •

RELIGION AND BELIEFS:

Religion played a central role in Mauretanian life, with the worship of a pantheon of gods and goddesses similar to those of ancient Rome and Carthage. The most important deity was Baal Hammon, the god of fertility and agriculture, who was venerated as the patron deity of the Mauretanian rulers. Other important gods included Tanit, the goddess of love and war, and Melqart, the god of the sea and commerce. The Mauretanian religion also included elements of indigenous Berber beliefs, such as ancestor worship and nature reverence.

Decline and Legacy:

The decline of the Kingdom of Mauretania began in the 3rd century AD, as external pressures, internal conflicts, and the decline of trade routes weakened its position. The kingdom's vulnerability was exploited by neighboring powers, including the Roman Empire and the emerging Christian kingdoms of North Africa, who launched military campaigns against Mauretania in the late antiquity period. By the 5th century AD, Mauretania had been reduced to a shadow of its former glory, eventually succumbing to conquest and assimilation by the Byzantine Empire and the Vandals.

Despite its decline, the Kingdom of Mauretania left a lasting legacy that continues to shape the culture and history of North Africa and the Mediterranean world. Its monumental architecture, sophisticated urban centers, and cultural achievements are a testament to the ingenuity, resilience, and enduring spirit of one of the ancient world's most remarkable civilizations. The legacy of the Kingdom of Mauretania lives on in the archaeological sites, artifacts, and oral traditions of the region, serving as a source of inspiration and pride for generations to come.

The Blemmyes Kingdom, also known as the Blemmyes State or simply Blemmyia, was an ancient civilization located in the Nile Valley region of present-day Sudan and Egypt. Flourishing from approximately the 3rd century BC to the 4th century AD, the Blemmyes Kingdom was a significant political and cultural power in northeastern Africa. In this essay, we will explore the history, economy, society, culture, governance, religion, architecture, and legacy of the Blemmyes Kingdom.

• • • •

ORIGINS AND EARLY HISTORY:

The origins of the Blemmyes Kingdom can be traced back to the indigenous peoples of the Nile Valley, particularly the Blemmyes tribe, who inhabited the region since ancient times. The Blemmyes were a nomadic people known for their warrior culture and pastoral way of life. Over time, the Blemmyes established a sedentary lifestyle, settling in villages and towns along the Nile River and its tributaries.

• • • •

RISE TO POWER:

The Blemmyes Kingdom reached its zenith during the Hellenistic period, when it became a major player in regional politics and trade. Under the influence of Greek and Roman cultural influences, the Blemmyes adopted new technologies, institutions, and ideas that transformed their society. The kingdom's strategic location along the Nile facilitated trade and cultural exchange with neighboring civilizations, including Egypt, Nubia, and the Red Sea coast.

• • • •

ECONOMY AND TRADE:

The economy of the Blemmyes Kingdom was based primarily on agriculture, with the cultivation of crops such as wheat, barley, millet, and sorghum supporting a growing population. The fertile soil of the Nile Valley and the region's access to water resources facilitated agriculture and allowed for the development of urban centers and settlements. Additionally, the kingdom controlled important trade routes linking sub-Saharan Africa with the Mediterranean world, enabling the exchange of goods such as ivory, gold, incense, and spices.

• • • •

SOCIETY AND CULTURE:

Blemmyes society was hierarchical, with a ruling class of nobles, priests, and military leaders overseeing the administration of the kingdom. Below them were artisans, merchants, farmers, and laborers, while slaves performed menial tasks. The Blemmyes people were skilled craftsmen, known for their pottery, jewelry, textiles, and metalwork. They also excelled in the production of monumental architecture, with temples, palaces, and fortifications serving as symbols of royal power and religious devotion.

• • • •

GOVERNANCE AND ADMINISTRATION:

The Blemmyes Kingdom was governed by a centralized monarchy, with power concentrated in the hands of the king, or "Blemmyes." The Blemmyes ruled from the royal capital and exercised authority over a network of provincial governors, known as "kings of the land." Local governance was facilitated by a system of tributary states and client kingdoms, which paid homage to the Blemmyes in exchange for protection and trade privileges. The kingdom's legal system was based on customary law and Blemmyes traditions, with judges and councils presiding over disputes and grievances.

• • • •

RELIGION AND BELIEFS:

Religion played a central role in Blemmyes life, with the worship of a pantheon of gods and goddesses similar to those of ancient Egypt and Nubia. The most important deity was Amun, the god of the sun and kingship, who was venerated as the patron deity of the Blemmyes rulers. Other important gods included Osiris, Isis, Horus, and Anubis, whose cults flourished in Blemmyes temples and sanctuaries. The Blemmyes religion also included elements of indigenous African beliefs, such as ancestor worship and nature reverence.

Decline and Legacy:

The decline of the Blemmyes Kingdom began in the 4th century AD, as external pressures, internal conflicts, and the decline of trade routes weakened its position. The kingdom's vulnerability was exploited by neighboring powers, including the Roman Empire and the emerging Christian kingdoms of North Africa, who launched military campaigns against the Blemmyes in the late antiquity period. By the 5th century AD, the Blemmyes Kingdom had been reduced to a shadow of its former glory, eventually succumbing to conquest and assimilation by the Byzantine Empire and the Arab Caliphates.

Despite its decline, the Blemmyes Kingdom left a lasting legacy that continues to shape the culture and history of Sudan and Egypt. Its monumental architecture, sophisticated urban centers, and cultural achievements are a testament to the ingenuity, resilience, and enduring spirit of one of northeastern Africa's most remarkable civilizations. The legacy of the Blemmyes Kingdom lives on in the archaeological sites, artifacts, and oral traditions of the region, serving as a source of inspiration and pride for generations to come.

Kingdom of Zimbabwe

The Kingdom of Zimbabwe, also known as the Great Zimbabwe Empire, was a medieval civilization located in present-day Zimbabwe, southern Africa. Flourishing from approximately the 11th to the 15th century AD, the Kingdom of Zimbabwe was one of the most significant and influential civilizations in the region. In this essay, we will explore the history, economy, society, culture, governance, religion, architecture, and legacy of the Kingdom of Zimbabwe.

• • • •

ORIGINS AND EARLY HISTORY:

The origins of the Kingdom of Zimbabwe can be traced back to the Shona people, who migrated into the region from the north and settled in the plateau areas of present-day Zimbabwe. Over time, these settlers established a network of agricultural communities and trade routes, laying the foundations for the development of a centralized state. The rise of Zimbabwe as a political entity coincided with the decline of earlier civilizations in the region, such as Mapungubwe and Khami.

• • • •

RISE TO POWER:

Zimbabwe reached its zenith during the 13th and 14th centuries AD when it became a major center of trade, culture, and political power in southern Africa. Under the leadership of its rulers, Zimbabwe expanded its territory through conquest and alliance-building, establishing a network of tributary states and client kingdoms. The kingdom's strategic location at the crossroads of trade routes linking the interior of southern Africa with the Indian Ocean facilitated commerce and cultural exchange with neighboring civilizations, including the Swahili coast, Great Zimbabwe, and the Limpopo Valley.

. . . .

ECONOMY AND TRADE:

The economy of the Kingdom of Zimbabwe was based primarily on agriculture, with the cultivation of crops such as millet, sorghum, maize, and beans supporting a growing population. Zimbabwe's access to fertile soil and reliable water sources facilitated agriculture and allowed for the development of urban centers and settlements. Additionally, the kingdom controlled important trade routes linking southern Africa with the Indian Ocean, enabling the exchange of goods such as ivory, gold, copper, iron, ceramics, and glass beads.

. . . .

SOCIETY AND CULTURE:

Zimbabwean society was hierarchical, with a ruling class of nobles, priests, and military leaders overseeing the administration of the kingdom. Below them were artisans, merchants, farmers, and laborers, while slaves performed menial tasks. The Zimbabwean people were skilled craftsmen, known for their pottery, jewelry, textiles, and metalwork. They also excelled in the production of monumental architecture, with the Great Zimbabwe complex serving as the royal capital and religious center of the kingdom.

. . . .

GOVERNANCE AND ADMINISTRATION:

The Kingdom of Zimbabwe was governed by a centralized monarchy, with power concentrated in the hands of the king, or "Zimbabwe." The Zimbabwe ruled from the royal capital and exercised authority over a network of provincial governors, known as "lords of the land." Local governance was facilitated by a system of tributary states and client kingdoms, which paid homage to the Zimbabwe in exchange for protection and trade privileges. The kingdom's legal system was based on customary law and Zimbabwean traditions, with councils and elders presiding over disputes and grievances.

• • • •

RELIGION AND BELIEFS:

Religion played a central role in Zimbabwean life, with the worship of ancestral spirits and natural forces such as the sun, moon, and rain. The most important deity was Mwari, the supreme god of the Shona pantheon, who was venerated as the creator of the universe and the protector of the Zimbabwean rulers. Other important religious practices included ancestor worship, divination, and ritual sacrifice. Zimbabwean religious beliefs were closely intertwined with the kingdom's social structure, political organization, and cultural identity.

• • • •

DECLINE AND LEGACY:

The decline of the Kingdom of Zimbabwe began in the 15th century AD, as external pressures, internal conflicts, and environmental changes weakened its position. The kingdom's vulnerability was exploited by neighboring powers, including the rising states of the Mutapa Empire and the Portuguese explorers, who sought to control the region's trade routes and resources. By the 16th century AD, Zimbabwe had been abandoned, eventually succumbing to conquest and assimilation by the neighboring kingdoms and European colonial powers.

Despite its decline, the Kingdom of Zimbabwe left a lasting legacy that continues to shape the culture and history of southern Africa. Its monumental architecture, sophisticated urban centers, and cultural achievements are a testament to the ingenuity, resilience, and enduring spirit of one of Africa's most remarkable civilizations. The legacy of the Kingdom of Zimbabwe lives on in the archaeological sites, artifacts, and oral traditions of the region, serving as a source of inspiration and pride for generations to come.

Ife Kingdom

The Ife Kingdom, also known as the Kingdom of Ife, was an ancient civilization located in present-day southwestern Nigeria. Flourishing from approximately the 4th century AD to the 15th century AD, Ife was a center of art, culture, and political power in West Africa. In this essay, we will explore the history, economy, society, culture, governance, religion, architecture, and legacy of the Ife Kingdom.

. . . .

ORIGINS AND EARLY HISTORY:

The origins of the Ife Kingdom are shrouded in myth and legend, with oral traditions tracing its founding to divine beings and mythical ancestors. According to Yoruba mythology, Ife was the birthplace of humanity and the spiritual center of the universe. The Ife people believed that their city was founded by the god Oduduwa, who descended from the heavens to establish civilization on earth. Over time, Ife evolved into a prosperous and cosmopolitan kingdom, renowned for its artistic achievements and cultural traditions.

. . . .

RISE TO POWER:

Ife reached its zenith during the medieval period when it became a major center of trade, culture, and political authority in West Africa. Under the leadership of its rulers, Ife expanded its territory through conquest and alliance-building, establishing a network of tributary states and client kingdoms. The kingdom's strategic location in the heart of the Yoruba homeland facilitated commerce and cultural exchange with neighboring civilizations, including Benin, Oyo, and Dahomey.

• • • •

ECONOMY AND TRADE:

The economy of the Ife Kingdom was based primarily on agriculture, with the cultivation of crops such as yams, cassava, millet, and beans supporting a growing population. Ife's access to fertile soil and abundant rainfall in the rainforest region of Nigeria facilitated agriculture and allowed for the development of urban centers and settlements. Additionally, the kingdom controlled important trade routes linking West Africa with the trans-Saharan trade network, enabling the exchange of goods such as gold, ivory, kola nuts, and slaves.

• • • •

SOCIETY AND CULTURE:

Ife society was hierarchical, with a ruling class of kings, chiefs, priests, and warriors overseeing the administration of the kingdom. Below them were artisans, merchants, farmers, and laborers, while slaves performed menial tasks. The Ife people were renowned for their artistic achievements, particularly in the fields of sculpture, pottery, and metalwork. Ife artists created exquisite works of art depicting human figures, animals, and mythical beings, which served as symbols of royal power and religious significance.

• • • •

GOVERNANCE AND ADMINISTRATION:

The Kingdom of Ife was governed by a centralized monarchy, with power concentrated in the hands of the king, or "Oba." The Oba ruled from the royal palace and exercised authority over a network of provincial governors, known as "Obas of the land." Local governance was facilitated by a system of tributary states and client kingdoms, which paid homage to the Oba in exchange for protection and trade privileges. The kingdom's legal system was based on customary law and Ife traditions, with councils and elders presiding over disputes and grievances.

• • • •

RELIGION AND BELIEFS:

Religion played a central role in Ife life, with the worship of a pantheon of gods and goddesses representing various aspects of the natural world and human experience. The most important deity was Oduduwa, the creator god and mythical ancestor of the Ife people, who was venerated as the progenitor of kingship and civilization. Other important gods included Ogun, the god of iron and warfare, and Osun, the goddess of fertility and rivers. Ife religious beliefs were expressed through rituals, ceremonies, and festivals honoring the gods and ancestors.

Decline and Legacy:

The decline of the Kingdom of Ife began in the 15th century AD, as external pressures, internal conflicts, and the rise of rival states weakened its position. The kingdom's vulnerability was exploited by neighboring powers, including the emerging Oyo Empire and the European colonial powers, who sought to control the region's trade routes and resources. By the 16th century AD, Ife had been eclipsed by the rise of other Yoruba kingdoms, eventually succumbing to conquest and assimilation by the Oyo Empire.

Despite its decline, the Kingdom of Ife left a lasting legacy that continues to shape the culture and history of Nigeria and the broader Yoruba-speaking world. Its artistic achievements, cultural traditions, and political institutions are a testament to the ingenuity, resilience, and enduring spirit of one of Africa's most remarkable civilizations. The legacy of the Kingdom of Ife lives on in the archaeological sites, artifacts, and oral traditions of the region, serving as a source of inspiration and pride for generations to come.

The Benin Empire, also known as the Edo Empire, was an ancient civilization located in present-day southern Nigeria. Flourishing from approximately the 11th century AD to the late 19th century AD, the Benin Empire was one of the most powerful and advanced states in West Africa. In this essay, we will explore the history, economy, society, culture, governance, religion, architecture, and legacy of the Benin Empire.

Origins and Early History:

The origins of the Benin Empire can be traced back to the Edo people, who migrated into the region from the savannahs of the Niger Delta and settled in the rainforest area of present-day Nigeria. Over time, these settlers established a network of agricultural communities and trade routes, laying the foundations for the development of a centralized state. The rise of Benin as a political entity coincided with the decline of earlier civilizations in the region, such as Ife and Oyo.

Rise to Power:

Benin reached its zenith during the medieval period when it became a major center of trade, culture, and political authority in West Africa. Under the leadership of its rulers, Benin expanded its territory through conquest and alliance-building, establishing a network of tributary states and client kingdoms. The kingdom's strategic location in the Niger Delta facilitated commerce and cultural exchange with neighboring civilizations, including Yoruba, Igbo, and Hausa-Fulani.

• • • •

ECONOMY AND TRADE:

The economy of the Benin Empire was based primarily on agriculture, with the cultivation of crops such as yams, cassava, maize, and palm oil supporting a growing population. Benin's access to fertile soil and abundant rainfall in the rainforest region of Nigeria facilitated agriculture and allowed for the development of urban centers and settlements. Additionally, the kingdom controlled important trade routes linking West Africa with the trans-Saharan trade network, enabling the exchange of goods such as ivory, gold, pepper, and slaves.

Society and Culture:

Benin society was hierarchical, with a ruling class of kings, chiefs, priests, and warriors overseeing the administration of the kingdom. Below them were artisans, merchants, farmers, and laborers, while slaves performed menial tasks. The Benin people were renowned for their artistic achievements, particularly in the fields of sculpture, pottery, and metallurgy. Benin artists created exquisite works of art depicting human figures, animals, and mythical beings, which served as symbols of royal power and religious significance.

Governance and Administration:

The Benin Empire was governed by a centralized monarchy, with power concentrated in the hands of the Oba, or king. The Oba ruled from the royal palace and exercised authority over a network of provincial governors, known as "Enogies." Local governance was facilitated by a system of tributary states and client kingdoms, which paid homage to the Oba in exchange for protection and trade privileges. The kingdom's legal system was based on customary law and Benin traditions, with councils and elders presiding over disputes and grievances.

• • • •

RELIGION AND BELIEFS:

Religion played a central role in Benin life, with the worship of a pantheon of gods and goddesses representing various aspects of the natural world and human experience. The most important deity was Olokun, the god of the sea and wealth, who was venerated as the protector of the Benin rulers and the patron of commerce and prosperity. Other important gods included Ogun, the god of iron and warfare, and Osun, the goddess of fertility and rivers. Benin religious beliefs were expressed through rituals, ceremonies, and festivals honoring the gods and ancestors.

Decline and Legacy:

The decline of the Benin Empire began in the late 19th century AD, as external pressures, internal conflicts, and the rise of European colonial powers weakened its position. The kingdom's vulnerability was exploited by the British Empire, who launched a series of military campaigns against Benin in the late 19th and early 20th centuries. In 1897, British forces sacked the royal palace of Benin and looted its treasures, effectively bringing an end to the empire.

Despite its decline, the Benin Empire left a lasting legacy that continues to shape the culture and history of Nigeria and the broader West African region. Its artistic achievements, cultural traditions, and political institutions are a testament to the ingenuity, resilience, and enduring spirit of one of Africa's most remarkable civilizations. The legacy of the Benin Empire lives on in the archaeological sites, artifacts, and oral traditions of the region, serving as a source of inspiration and pride for generations to come.

The Oyo Empire, also known as the Oyo Kingdom, was a powerful and influential civilization located in present-day southwestern Nigeria. Flourishing from approximately the 15th century AD to the early 19th century AD, the Oyo Empire was one of the largest and most organized states in West Africa. In this essay, we will explore the history, economy, society, culture, governance, religion, architecture, and legacy of the Oyo Empire.

Origins and Early History:

The origins of the Oyo Empire can be traced back to the Yoruba people, who migrated into the region from the savannahs of the Niger Delta and settled in the forests and grasslands of present-day Nigeria. Over time, these settlers established a network of agricultural communities and trade routes, laying the foundations for the development of a centralized state. The rise of Oyo as a political entity coincided with the decline of earlier civilizations in the region, such as Ife and Benin.

. . . .

RISE TO POWER:

Oyo reached its zenith during the 17th and 18th centuries when it became a major center of trade, culture, and political authority in West Africa. Under the leadership of its rulers, Oyo expanded its territory through conquest and alliance-building, establishing a network of tributary states and client kingdoms. The kingdom's strategic location in the heart of the Yoruba homeland facilitated commerce and cultural exchange with neighboring civilizations, including Benin, Dahomey, and the trans-Saharan trade network.

. . . .

ECONOMY AND TRADE:

The economy of the Oyo Empire was based primarily on agriculture, with the cultivation of crops such as yams, cassava, millet, and maize supporting a growing population. Oyo's access to fertile soil and reliable rainfall in the forest and savannah regions of Nigeria facilitated agriculture and allowed for the development of urban centers and settlements. Additionally, the kingdom controlled important trade routes linking West Africa with the trans-Saharan trade network, enabling the exchange of goods such as ivory, kola nuts, slaves, and textiles.

....

SOCIETY AND CULTURE:

Oyo society was hierarchical, with a ruling class of kings, chiefs, priests, and warriors overseeing the administration of the empire. Below them were artisans, merchants, farmers, and laborers, while slaves performed menial tasks. The Oyo people were known for their artistic achievements, particularly in the fields of sculpture, pottery, and textiles. Oyo artists created intricate works of art depicting human figures, animals, and mythical beings, which served as symbols of royal power and religious significance.

....

GOVERNANCE AND ADMINISTRATION:

The Oyo Empire was governed by a centralized monarchy, with power concentrated in the hands of the Alaafin, or king. The Alaafin ruled from the royal palace and exercised authority over a network of provincial governors, known as "Obas." Local governance was facilitated by a system of tributary states and client kingdoms, which paid homage to the Alaafin in exchange for protection and trade privileges. The kingdom's legal system was based on customary law and

Oyo traditions, with councils and elders presiding over disputes and grievances.

• • • •

RELIGION AND BELIEFS:

Religion played a central role in Oyo life, with the worship of a pantheon of gods and goddesses representing various aspects of the natural world and human experience. The most important deity was Orunmila, the god of wisdom and divination, who was venerated as the patron of kingship and justice. Other important gods included Ogun, the god of iron and warfare, and Osun, the goddess of fertility and rivers. Oyo religious beliefs were expressed through rituals, ceremonies, and festivals honoring the gods and ancestors.

• • • •

DECLINE AND LEGACY:

The decline of the Oyo Empire began in the early 19th century AD, as external pressures, internal conflicts, and the rise of European colonial powers weakened its position. The empire's vulnerability was exploited by rival states, including the emerging Fulani jihad and the British Empire, who sought to control the region's trade routes and resources. By the late 19th century AD, Oyo had been fragmented and weakened, eventually succumbing to conquest and colonization by the British.

Despite its decline, the Oyo Empire left a lasting legacy that continues to shape the culture and history of Nigeria and the broader West African region. Its political institutions, legal systems, and cultural traditions are a testament to the ingenuity, resilience, and enduring spirit of one of Africa's most remarkable civilizations. The legacy of the Oyo Empire lives on in the archaeological sites, artifacts, and oral traditions of the region, serving as a source of inspiration and pride for generations to come.

Kanem Empire

The Kanem Empire, also known as the Kanem-Bornu Empire, was a medieval civilization located in present-day Chad, Nigeria, Cameroon, and Niger. Flourishing from approximately the 9th century AD to the 19th century AD, the Kanem Empire was one of the longest-lasting states in the history of West Africa. In this essay, we will explore the history, economy, society, culture, governance, religion, architecture, and legacy of the Kanem Empire.

Origins and Early History:

The origins of the Kanem Empire can be traced back to the Kanembu people, who were a mixture of indigenous Saharan populations and immigrant Arab-Berber groups. The Kanembu settled in the Lake Chad basin region and established a network of agricultural communities and trade routes. The rise of Kanem as a political entity coincided with the decline of earlier civilizations in the region, such as the Sao and the Kanuri.

• • • •

RISE TO POWER:

Kanem reached its zenith during the medieval period when it became a major center of trade, culture, and political authority in the Sahel region of West Africa. Under the leadership of its rulers, Kanem expanded its territory through conquest and alliance-building, establishing a network of tributary states and client kingdoms. The empire's strategic location at the crossroads of trans-Saharan trade routes facilitated commerce and cultural exchange with neighboring civilizations, including Mali, Songhai, and the Hausa city-states.

• • • •

ECONOMY AND TRADE:

The economy of the Kanem Empire was based primarily on agriculture, with the cultivation of crops such as millet, sorghum, wheat, and dates supporting a growing population. Kanem's access to fertile soil and reliable water sources in the Lake Chad basin facilitated agriculture and allowed for the development of urban centers and settlements. Additionally, the empire controlled important trade routes linking West Africa with North Africa and the Mediterranean world, enabling the exchange of goods such as salt, gold, slaves, ivory, and horses.

• • • •

SOCIETY AND CULTURE:

Kanem society was hierarchical, with a ruling class of kings, nobles, and bureaucrats overseeing the administration of the empire. Below them were artisans, merchants, farmers, and laborers, while slaves performed menial tasks. The Kanembu people were known for their artistic achievements, particularly in the fields of pottery, weaving, and metalwork. Kanem artisans created intricate works of art depicting human figures, animals, and geometric patterns, which served as symbols of royal power and cultural identity.

• • • •

GOVERNANCE AND ADMINISTRATION:

The Kanem Empire was governed by a centralized monarchy, with power concentrated in the hands of the Mai, or king. The Mai ruled from the royal palace and exercised authority over a network of provincial governors, known as "Galadima." Local governance was facilitated by a system of tributary states and client kingdoms, which paid homage to the Mai in exchange for protection and trade privileges. The empire's legal system was based on Islamic law and Kanembu traditions, with judges and councils presiding over disputes and grievances.

Religion and Beliefs:

Religion played a central role in Kanem life, with Islam serving as the dominant faith of the ruling elite and urban population. The conversion to Islam began in the 11th century AD under the influence of Muslim traders and scholars from North Africa and the Middle East. However, traditional African religious beliefs and practices persisted among rural communities and indigenous peoples, who worshipped a pantheon of gods and spirits representing various aspects of the natural world and human experience.

• • • •

DECLINE AND LEGACY:

The decline of the Kanem Empire began in the 19th century AD, as external pressures, internal conflicts, and the rise of European colonial powers weakened its position. The empire's vulnerability was exploited by rival states, including the Sokoto Caliphate and the French Empire, who sought to control the region's trade routes and resources. By the late 19th century AD, Kanem had been fragmented and weakened, eventually succumbing to conquest and colonization by the French.

Despite its decline, the Kanem Empire left a lasting legacy that continues to shape the culture and history of Chad, Nigeria, Cameroon, and Niger. Its political institutions, legal systems, and cultural traditions are a testament to the ingenuity, resilience, and enduring spirit of one of Africa's most remarkable civilizations. The legacy of the Kanem Empire lives on in the archaeological sites, artifacts, and oral traditions of the region, serving as a source of inspiration and pride for generations to come.

The Ashanti Empire, also known as the Asante Empire, was a powerful and influential civilization located in present-day Ghana, West Africa. Flourishing from approximately the late 17th century AD to the late 19th century AD, the Ashanti Empire was one of the most formidable states in the region, known for its military prowess, political organization, and rich cultural heritage. In this essay, we will explore the history, economy, society, culture, governance, religion, architecture, and legacy of the Ashanti Empire.

Origins and Early History:

The origins of the Ashanti Empire can be traced back to the Ashanti people, who were part of the Akan ethnic group that migrated into the region from the north. The Ashanti settled in the forested areas of present-day Ghana and established a network of agricultural communities and trade routes. The rise of the Ashanti as a political entity coincided with the decline of earlier civilizations in the region, such as the Denkyira and the Akwamu.

· · · ·

RISE TO POWER:

The Ashanti Empire reached its zenith during the 18th and 19th centuries when it became a major center of trade, culture, and political authority in West Africa. Under the leadership of its rulers, the Ashanti expanded their territory through conquest and alliance-building, establishing a network of tributary states and client kingdoms. The empire's strategic location in the Gold Coast region facilitated commerce and cultural exchange with neighboring civilizations, including the Fante, the Ga-Dangme, and European colonial powers.

Economy and Trade:

The economy of the Ashanti Empire was based primarily on agriculture, with the cultivation of crops such as cocoa, yams, plantains, and cassava supporting a growing population. The Ashanti's access to fertile soil and abundant rainfall in the forest region of Ghana facilitated agriculture and allowed for the development of urban centers and settlements. Additionally, the empire controlled important trade routes linking West Africa with Europe and the Americas, enabling the exchange of goods such as gold, slaves, ivory, and textiles.

• • • •

SOCIETY AND CULTURE:

Ashanti society was hierarchical, with a ruling class of kings, chiefs, and nobles overseeing the administration of the empire. Below them were artisans, merchants, farmers, and laborers, while slaves performed menial tasks. The Ashanti people were known for their artistic achievements, particularly in the fields of weaving, pottery, and metalwork. Ashanti artisans created exquisite works of art depicting human figures, animals, and geometric patterns, which served as symbols of royal power and cultural identity.

• • • •

GOVERNANCE AND ADMINISTRATION:

The Ashanti Empire was governed by a centralized monarchy, with power concentrated in the hands of the Asantehene, or king. The Asantehene ruled from the royal palace in Kumasi and exercised authority over a network of provincial governors, known as "Omanhene." Local governance was facilitated by a system of tributary states and client kingdoms, which paid homage to the Asantehene in exchange for protection and trade privileges. The empire's legal system was based on customary law and Ashanti traditions, with councils and elders presiding over disputes and grievances.

Religion and Beliefs:

Religion played a central role in Ashanti life, with the worship of a pantheon of gods and goddesses representing various aspects of the natural world and human experience. The most important deity was Nyame, the supreme god of the Ashanti pantheon, who was venerated as the creator of the universe and the source of all life. Other important gods included Anansi, the trickster god, and Asase Yaa, the earth goddess. Ashanti religious beliefs were expressed through rituals, ceremonies, and festivals honoring the gods and ancestors.

Decline and Legacy:

The decline of the Ashanti Empire began in the late 19th century AD, as external pressures, internal conflicts, and the rise of European colonial powers weakened its position. The empire's vulnerability was exploited by rival states, including the British Empire, who launched a series of military campaigns against the Ashanti in the 19th century. In 1900, British forces captured Kumasi and deposed the Asantehene, effectively bringing an end to the empire.

Despite its decline, the Ashanti Empire left a lasting legacy that continues to shape the culture and history of Ghana and the broader West African region. Its political institutions, legal systems, and cultural traditions are a testament to the ingenuity, resilience, and enduring spirit of one of Africa's most remarkable civilizations. The legacy of the Ashanti Empire lives on in the archaeological sites, artifacts, and oral traditions of the region, serving as a source of inspiration and pride for generations to come.

Dahomey Empire

The Dahomey Empire, also known as the Kingdom of Dahomey, was a powerful and influential civilization located in present-day Benin, West Africa. Flourishing from approximately the 17th century AD to the late 19th century AD, the Dahomey Empire was one of the most formidable states in the region, known for its military prowess, political organization, and unique cultural practices. In this essay, we will explore the history, economy, society, culture, governance, religion, architecture, and legacy of the Dahomey Empire.

. . . .

ORIGINS AND EARLY HISTORY:

The origins of the Dahomey Empire can be traced back to the Fon people, who migrated into the region from the savannahs of northern Nigeria and settled in the coastal areas of present-day Benin. The Fon established a network of agricultural communities and trade routes, laying the foundations for the development of a centralized state. The rise of Dahomey as a political entity coincided with the decline of neighboring kingdoms, such as Allada and Ouidah.

Rise to Power:

Dahomey reached its zenith during the 18th and 19th centuries when it became a major center of trade, culture, and political authority in West Africa. Under the leadership of its rulers, Dahomey expanded its territory through conquest and alliance-building, establishing a network of tributary states and client kingdoms. The empire's strategic location on the Gulf of Guinea facilitated commerce and cultural exchange with neighboring civilizations, including the Yoruba, the Aja, and European colonial powers.

• • • •

ECONOMY AND TRADE:

The economy of the Dahomey Empire was based primarily on agriculture, with the cultivation of crops such as yams, cassava, maize, and palm oil supporting a growing population. Dahomey's access to fertile soil and abundant rainfall in the coastal region of Benin facilitated agriculture and allowed for the development of urban centers and settlements. Additionally, the empire controlled important trade routes linking West Africa with Europe and the Americas, enabling the exchange of goods such as slaves, ivory, textiles, and firearms.

Society and Culture:

Dahomey society was hierarchical, with a ruling class of kings, nobles, and warriors overseeing the administration of the empire. Below them were artisans, merchants, farmers, and laborers, while slaves performed menial tasks. The Dahomey people were known for their artistic achievements, particularly in the fields of sculpture, pottery, and weaving. Dahomey artisans created exquisite works of art depicting human figures, animals, and mythical beings, which served as symbols of royal power and cultural identity.

• • • •

GOVERNANCE AND ADMINISTRATION:

The Dahomey Empire was governed by a centralized monarchy, with power concentrated in the hands of the king, or "Oba." The Oba ruled from the royal palace in Abomey and exercised authority over a network of provincial governors, known as "Agas." Local governance was facilitated by a system of tributary states and client kingdoms, which paid homage to the Oba in exchange for protection and trade privileges. The empire's legal system was based on customary law and Dahomey traditions, with councils and elders presiding over disputes and grievances.

Religion and Beliefs:

Religion played a central role in Dahomey life, with the worship of a pantheon of gods and goddesses representing various aspects of the natural world and human experience. The most important deity was Mawu-Lisa, the supreme god of the Dahomey pantheon, who was venerated as the creator of the universe and the source of all life. Other important gods included Legba, the messenger god, and Gbadu, the earth goddess. Dahomey religious beliefs were expressed through rituals, ceremonies, and festivals honoring the gods and ancestors.

• • • •

DECLINE AND LEGACY:

The decline of the Dahomey Empire began in the late 19th century AD, as external pressures, internal conflicts, and the abolition of the transatlantic slave trade weakened its position. The empire's vulnerability was exploited by European colonial powers, particularly the French, who launched a series of military campaigns against Dahomey in the late 19th and early 20th centuries. In 1894, French forces captured Abomey and deposed the last king of Dahomey, effectively bringing an end to the empire.

Despite its decline, the Dahomey Empire left a lasting legacy that continues to shape the culture and history of Benin and the broader West African region. Its political institutions, military traditions, and cultural practices are a testament to the ingenuity, resilience, and enduring spirit of one of Africa's most remarkable civilizations. The legacy of the Dahomey Empire lives on in the archaeological sites, artifacts, and oral traditions of the region, serving as a source of inspiration and pride for generations to come.

Kingdom of Kongo

The Kingdom of Kongo, also known as the Kongo Empire or the Kingdom of Bakongo, was a powerful and influential civilization located in central Africa, encompassing parts of present-day Angola, the Democratic Republic of Congo, and the Republic of Congo. Flourishing from approximately the 14th century AD to the late 19th century AD, the Kingdom of Kongo was one of the largest and most organized states in sub-Saharan Africa. In this essay, we will explore the history, economy, society, culture, governance, religion, architecture, and legacy of the Kingdom of Kongo.

. . . .

ORIGINS AND EARLY HISTORY:

The origins of the Kingdom of Kongo can be traced back to the Kongo people, who were part of the Bantu-speaking populations that migrated into the region from the northeast. The Kongo settled in the fertile lowlands along the Congo River and established a network of agricultural communities and trade routes. The rise of the Kingdom of Kongo as a political entity coincided with the decline of earlier civilizations in the region, such as the Luba and the Lunda.

Rise to Power:

The Kingdom of Kongo reached its zenith during the 15th and 16th centuries when it became a major center of trade, culture, and political authority in Central Africa. Under the leadership of its rulers, Kongo expanded its territory through conquest and alliance-building, establishing a network of tributary states and client kingdoms. The kingdom's strategic location along the Congo River facilitated commerce and cultural exchange with neighboring civilizations, including the Lunda, the Luba, and Portuguese traders.

• • • •

ECONOMY AND TRADE:

The economy of the Kingdom of Kongo was based primarily on agriculture, with the cultivation of crops such as maize, cassava, millet, and palm oil supporting a growing population. Kongo's access to fertile soil and reliable rainfall in the Congo basin facilitated agriculture and allowed for the development of urban centers and settlements. Additionally, the kingdom controlled important trade routes linking Central Africa with the Atlantic coast, enabling the exchange of goods such as ivory, copper, salt, slaves, and European manufactured goods.

Society and Culture:

Kongo society was hierarchical, with a ruling class of kings, nobles, and courtiers overseeing the administration of the kingdom. Below them were artisans, merchants, farmers, and laborers, while slaves performed menial tasks. The Kongo people were known for their artistic achievements, particularly in the fields of sculpture, pottery, and weaving. Kongo artisans created intricate works of art depicting human figures, animals, and geometric patterns, which served as symbols of royal power and cultural identity.

• • • •

GOVERNANCE AND ADMINISTRATION:

The Kingdom of Kongo was governed by a centralized monarchy, with power concentrated in the hands of the Manikongo, or king. The Manikongo ruled from the capital city of Mbanza Kongo and exercised authority over a network of provincial governors, known as "Ntinu." Local governance was facilitated by a system of tributary states and client kingdoms, which paid homage to the Manikongo in exchange for protection and trade privileges. The kingdom's legal system was based on customary law and Kongo traditions, with councils and elders presiding over disputes and grievances.

• • • •

RELIGION AND BELIEFS:

Religion played a central role in Kongo life, with the worship of a pantheon of gods and spirits representing various aspects of the natural world and human experience. The most important deity was Nzambi, the supreme god of the Kongo pantheon, who was venerated as the creator of the universe and the source of all life. Other important gods included Nzambi Mpungu, the sky god, and Nkuyu, the earth goddess. Kongo religious beliefs were expressed through rituals, ceremonies, and festivals honoring the gods and ancestors.

• • • •

DECLINE AND LEGACY:

The decline of the Kingdom of Kongo began in the late 16th century AD, as external pressures, internal conflicts, and the transatlantic slave trade weakened its position. The kingdom's vulnerability was exploited by European colonial powers, particularly the Portuguese, who established trade relations and later sought to conquer and colonize the region. By the late 19th century AD, Kongo had been fragmented and weakened, eventually succumbing to colonization by European powers.

Despite its decline, the Kingdom of Kongo left a lasting legacy that continues to shape the culture and history of Central Africa. Its political institutions, legal systems, and cultural practices are a testament to the ingenuity, resilience, and enduring spirit of one of Africa's most remarkable civilizations. The legacy of the Kingdom of Kongo lives on in the archaeological sites, artifacts, and oral traditions of the region, serving as a source of inspiration and pride for generations to come.

Mutapa Empire

The Mutapa Empire, also known as the Monomotapa Empire, was a powerful and influential civilization located in present-day Zimbabwe and Mozambique, in Southern Africa. Flourishing from approximately the 15th century AD to the late 19th century AD, the Mutapa Empire was one of the largest and most organized states in the region, known for its rich mineral resources, trade networks, and cultural achievements. In this essay, we will explore the history, economy, society, culture, governance, religion, architecture, and legacy of the Mutapa Empire.

. . . .

ORIGINS AND EARLY HISTORY:

The origins of the Mutapa Empire can be traced back to the Shona people, who migrated into the region from the north and settled in the highlands of present-day Zimbabwe. The Shona established a network of agricultural communities and trade routes, laying the foundations for the development of a centralized state. The rise of the Mutapa Empire as a political entity coincided with the decline of earlier civilizations in the region, such as Great Zimbabwe.

Rise to Power:

The Mutapa Empire reached its zenith during the 15th and 16th centuries when it became a major center of trade, culture, and political authority in Southern Africa. Under the leadership of its rulers, Mutapa expanded its territory through conquest and alliance-building, establishing a network of tributary states and client kingdoms. The empire's strategic location in the Zambezi River basin facilitated commerce and cultural exchange with neighboring civilizations, including the Portuguese, the Swahili city-states, and the Kingdom of Kongo.

Economy and Trade:

The economy of the Mutapa Empire was based primarily on agriculture and mining, with the cultivation of crops such as millet, sorghum, and maize supporting a growing population. Mutapa's access to fertile soil and reliable rainfall in the highlands of Zimbabwe facilitated agriculture and allowed for the development of urban centers and settlements. Additionally, the empire controlled important trade routes linking Southern Africa with the Indian Ocean and the Swahili coast, enabling the exchange of goods such as gold, ivory, copper, iron, and slaves.

Society and Culture:

Mutapa society was hierarchical, with a ruling class of kings, nobles, and warriors overseeing the administration of the empire. Below them were artisans, merchants, farmers, and laborers, while slaves performed menial tasks. The Mutapa people were known for their artistic achievements, particularly in the fields of sculpture, pottery, and weaving. Mutapa artisans created intricate works of art depicting human figures, animals, and geometric patterns, which served as symbols of royal power and cultural identity.

Governance and Administration:

The Mutapa Empire was governed by a centralized monarchy, with power concentrated in the hands of the Mwenemutapa, or king. The

Mwenemutapa ruled from the capital city of Great Zimbabwe and exercised authority over a network of provincial governors, known as "Zimbabwes." Local governance was facilitated by a system of tributary states and client kingdoms, which paid homage to the Mwenemutapa in exchange for protection and trade privileges. The empire's legal system was based on customary law and Mutapa traditions, with councils and elders presiding over disputes and grievances.

RELIGION AND BELIEFS:

Religion played a central role in Mutapa life, with the worship of a pantheon of gods and spirits representing various aspects of the natural world and human experience. The most important deity was Mwari, the supreme god of the Mutapa pantheon, who was venerated as the creator of the universe and the source of all life. Other important gods included the ancestors and spirits of nature. Mutapa religious beliefs were expressed through rituals, ceremonies, and festivals honoring the gods and ancestors.

DECLINE AND LEGACY:

The decline of the Mutapa Empire began in the late 17th century AD, as external pressures, internal conflicts, and the arrival of European colonial powers weakened its position. The empire's vulnerability was exploited by rival states, particularly the Portuguese, who sought to control the region's trade routes and resources. By the late 19th century AD, Mutapa had been fragmented and weakened, eventually succumbing to conquest and colonization by European powers.

Despite its decline, the Mutapa Empire left a lasting legacy that continues to shape the culture and history of Zimbabwe and Mozambique. Its political institutions, economic systems, and cultural traditions are a testament to the ingenuity, resilience, and enduring spirit of one of Africa's most remarkable civilizations. The legacy of the Mutapa Empire lives on in the archaeological sites, artifacts, and oral traditions of the region, serving as a source of inspiration and pride for generations to come.

Rozwi Empire

The Rozwi Empire, also known as the Rozwi Kingdom or the Rozwi State, was a powerful civilization located in present-day Zimbabwe, in Southern Africa. Flourishing from approximately the 15th century AD to the late 19th century AD, the Rozwi Empire was one of the most significant states in the region, known for its military strength, political organization, and cultural achievements. In this essay, we will explore the history, economy, society, culture, governance, religion, architecture, and legacy of the Rozwi Empire.

Origins and Early History:

The origins of the Rozwi Empire can be traced back to the Shona people, who migrated into the region from the north and settled in the highlands of present-day Zimbabwe. The Shona established a network of agricultural communities and trade routes, laying the foundations for the development of a centralized state. The rise of the Rozwi Empire as a political entity coincided with the decline of earlier civilizations in the region, such as Great Zimbabwe and the Mutapa Empire.

Rise to Power:

The Rozwi Empire reached its zenith during the 17th and 18th centuries when it became a major center of trade, culture, and political authority in Southern Africa. Under the leadership of its rulers, the Rozwi expanded their territory through conquest and alliance-building, establishing a network of tributary states and client kingdoms. The empire's strategic location in the Zambezi River basin facilitated commerce and cultural exchange with neighboring civilizations, including the Portuguese, the Swahili city-states, and the Kingdom of Kongo.

Economy and Trade:

The economy of the Rozwi Empire was based primarily on agriculture and mining, with the cultivation of crops such as millet, sorghum, and maize supporting a growing population. Rozwi's access to fertile soil and reliable rainfall in the highlands of Zimbabwe facilitated agriculture and allowed for the development of urban centers and settlements. Additionally, the empire controlled important trade routes linking Southern Africa with the Indian Ocean and the Swahili coast, enabling the exchange of goods such as gold, ivory, copper, iron, and slaves.

• • • •

SOCIETY AND CULTURE:

Rozwi society was hierarchical, with a ruling class of kings, nobles, and warriors overseeing the administration of the empire. Below them were artisans, merchants, farmers, and laborers, while slaves performed menial tasks. The Rozwi people were known for their artistic achievements, particularly in the fields of sculpture, pottery, and weaving. Rozwi artisans created intricate works of art depicting human figures, animals, and geometric patterns, which served as symbols of royal power and cultural identity.

• • • •

GOVERNANCE AND ADMINISTRATION:

The Rozwi Empire was governed by a centralized monarchy, with power concentrated in the hands of the Mambo, or king. The Mambo ruled from the capital city of Danangombe and exercised authority over a network of provincial governors, known as "Zimbabwes." Local governance was facilitated by a system of tributary states and client kingdoms, which paid homage to the Mambo in exchange for protection and trade privileges. The empire's legal system was based on customary law and Rozwi traditions, with councils and elders presiding over disputes and grievances.

Religion and Beliefs:

Religion played a central role in Rozwi life, with the worship of a pantheon of gods and spirits representing various aspects of the natural world and human experience. The most important deity was Mwari, the supreme god of the Rozwi pantheon, who was venerated as the creator of the universe and the source of all life. Other important gods included the ancestors and spirits of nature. Rozwi religious beliefs were expressed through rituals, ceremonies, and festivals honoring the gods and ancestors.

Decline and Legacy:

The decline of the Rozwi Empire began in the late 18th century AD, as external pressures, internal conflicts, and the arrival of European colonial powers weakened its position. The empire's vulnerability was exploited by rival states, particularly the Portuguese and the British, who sought to control the region's trade routes and resources. By the late 19th century AD, Rozwi had been fragmented and weakened, eventually succumbing to conquest and colonization by European powers.

Despite its decline, the Rozwi Empire left a lasting legacy that continues to shape the culture and history of Zimbabwe and Southern Africa. Its political institutions, economic systems, and cultural traditions are a testament to the ingenuity, resilience, and enduring spirit of one of Africa's most remarkable civilizations. The legacy of the Rozwi Empire lives on in the archaeological sites, artifacts, and oral traditions of the region, serving as a source of inspiration and pride for generations to come.

Kingdom of Luba

The Kingdom of Luba, also known as the Luba Empire, was a significant and influential civilization located in Central Africa, specifically in the region that is now part of the Democratic Republic of Congo. Flourishing from around the 15th century AD to the late 19th century AD, the Kingdom of Luba was renowned for its political organization, economic prosperity, and cultural achievements. In this essay, we will delve into the history, economy, society, culture, governance, religion, architecture, and legacy of the Kingdom of Luba.

Origins and Early History:

The origins of the Kingdom of Luba can be traced back to the Luba people, a Bantu-speaking ethnic group that migrated into the region from the north and settled in the savannah and forest areas of Central Africa. The Luba established a network of agricultural communities and trade routes, laying the foundations for the emergence of a centralized state. The rise of the Kingdom of Luba as a political entity coincided with the decline of earlier civilizations in the region, such as the Lunda and the Luba-Kasai.

Rise to Power:

The Kingdom of Luba reached its zenith during the 16th and 17th centuries when it became a major center of trade, culture, and political authority in Central Africa. Under the leadership of its rulers, Luba expanded its territory through conquest and alliance-building, establishing a network of tributary states and client kingdoms. The empire's strategic location in the Kasai River basin facilitated commerce and cultural exchange with neighboring civilizations, including the Kongo, the Lunda, and the Portuguese.

Economy and Trade:

The economy of the Kingdom of Luba was based primarily on agriculture, with the cultivation of crops such as millet, sorghum, maize, and cassava supporting a growing population. Luba's access to fertile soil and abundant rainfall in the Kasai region facilitated agriculture and allowed for the development of urban centers and settlements. Additionally, the empire controlled important trade routes linking Central Africa with the Atlantic coast, enabling the exchange of goods such as ivory, copper, salt, slaves, and European manufactured goods.

Society and Culture:

Luba society was hierarchical, with a ruling class of kings, nobles, and courtiers overseeing the administration of the empire. Below them were artisans, merchants, farmers, and laborers, while slaves performed menial tasks. The Luba people were known for their artistic achievements, particularly in the fields of sculpture, pottery, and weaving. Luba artisans created intricate works of art depicting human figures, animals, and geometric patterns, which served as symbols of royal power and cultural identity.

. . . .

GOVERNANCE AND ADMINISTRATION:

The Kingdom of Luba was governed by a centralized monarchy, with power concentrated in the hands of the Mwata, or king. The Mwata ruled from the capital city of Luba-Kasai and exercised authority over a network of provincial governors, known as "Balopwe." Local governance was facilitated by a system of tributary states and client kingdoms, which paid homage to the Mwata in exchange for protection and trade privileges. The empire's legal system was based on customary law and Luba traditions, with councils and elders presiding over disputes and grievances.

. . . .

RELIGION AND BELIEFS:

Religion played a central role in Luba life, with the worship of a pantheon of gods and spirits representing various aspects of the natural world and human experience. The most important deity was Kalonga, the supreme god of the Luba pantheon, who was venerated as the creator of the universe and the source of all life. Other important gods included the ancestors and spirits of nature. Luba religious beliefs were expressed through rituals, ceremonies, and festivals honoring the gods and ancestors.

Decline and Legacy:

The decline of the Kingdom of Luba began in the late 18th century AD, as external pressures, internal conflicts, and the arrival of European colonial powers weakened its position. The empire's vulnerability was exploited by rival states, particularly the Belgian Congo, which sought to control the region's trade routes and resources. By the late 19th century AD, Luba had been fragmented and weakened, eventually succumbing to conquest and colonization by European powers.

Despite its decline, the Kingdom of Luba left a lasting legacy that continues to shape the culture and history of the Democratic Republic of Congo and Central Africa. Its political institutions, economic systems, and cultural traditions are a testament to the ingenuity, resilience, and enduring spirit of one of Africa's most remarkable civilizations. The legacy of the Kingdom of Luba lives on in the archaeological sites, artifacts, and oral traditions of the region, serving as a source of inspiration and pride for generations to come.

The Kingdom of Lunda, also known as the Lunda Empire, was a significant and influential civilization located in Central and Southern Africa, specifically in the region that is now part of the Democratic Republic of Congo, Angola, and Zambia. Flourishing from approximately the 17th century AD to the late 19th century AD, the Kingdom of Lunda was renowned for its political organization, military strength, and cultural achievements. In this essay, we will explore the history, economy, society, culture, governance, religion, architecture, and legacy of the Kingdom of Lunda.

Origins and Early History:

The origins of the Kingdom of Lunda can be traced back to the Lunda people, a Bantu-speaking ethnic group that migrated into the region from the north and settled in the savannah and forest areas of Central Africa. The Lunda established a network of agricultural communities and trade routes, laying the foundations for the emergence of a centralized state. The rise of the Kingdom of Lunda as a political entity coincided with the decline of earlier civilizations in the region, such as the Luba and the Lunda-Kasai.

Rise to Power:

The Kingdom of Lunda reached its zenith during the 18th and 19th centuries when it became a major center of trade, culture, and political authority in Central and Southern Africa. Under the leadership of its rulers, Lunda expanded its territory through conquest and alliance-building, establishing a network of tributary states and client kingdoms. The empire's strategic location in the Zambezi River basin facilitated commerce and cultural exchange with neighboring civilizations, including the Luba, the Lunda, and the Portuguese.

· · · ·

ECONOMY AND TRADE:

The economy of the Kingdom of Lunda was based primarily on agriculture, with the cultivation of crops such as millet, sorghum, maize, and cassava supporting a growing population. Lunda's access to fertile soil and abundant rainfall in the Zambezi region facilitated agriculture and allowed for the development of urban centers and settlements. Additionally, the empire controlled important trade routes linking Central and Southern Africa with the Atlantic coast, enabling the exchange of goods such as ivory, copper, salt, slaves, and European manufactured goods.

• • • •

SOCIETY AND CULTURE:

Lunda society was hierarchical, with a ruling class of kings, nobles, and warriors overseeing the administration of the empire. Below them were artisans, merchants, farmers, and laborers, while slaves performed menial tasks. The Lunda people were known for their artistic achievements, particularly in the fields of sculpture, pottery, and weaving. Lunda artisans created intricate works of art depicting human figures, animals, and geometric patterns, which served as symbols of royal power and cultural identity.

• • • •

GOVERNANCE AND ADMINISTRATION:

The Kingdom of Lunda was governed by a centralized monarchy, with power concentrated in the hands of the Mwata, or king. The Mwata ruled from the capital city of Mwene Mutapa and exercised authority over a network of provincial governors, known as "Kazembe." Local governance was facilitated by a system of tributary states and client kingdoms, which paid homage to the Mwata in exchange for protection and trade privileges. The empire's legal system was based on customary law and Lunda traditions, with councils and elders presiding over disputes and grievances.

• • • •

RELIGION AND BELIEFS:

Religion played a central role in Lunda life, with the worship of a pantheon of gods and spirits representing various aspects of the natural world and human experience. The most important deity was Kalunga, the supreme god of the Lunda pantheon, who was venerated as the creator of the universe and the source of all life. Other important gods included the ancestors and spirits of nature. Lunda religious beliefs were expressed through rituals, ceremonies, and festivals honoring the gods and ancestors.

• • • •

DECLINE AND LEGACY:

The decline of the Kingdom of Lunda began in the late 19th century AD, as external pressures, internal conflicts, and the arrival of European colonial powers weakened its position. The empire's vulnerability was exploited by rival states, particularly the Portuguese and the British, who sought to control the region's trade routes and resources. By the late 19th century AD, Lunda had been fragmented and weakened, eventually succumbing to conquest and colonization by European powers.

Despite its decline, the Kingdom of Lunda left a lasting legacy that continues to shape the culture and history of the Democratic Republic of Congo, Angola, and Zambia. Its political institutions, economic systems, and cultural traditions are a testament to the ingenuity, resilience, and enduring spirit of one of Africa's most remarkable civilizations. The legacy of the Kingdom of Lunda lives on in the archaeological sites, artifacts, and oral traditions of the region, serving as a source of inspiration and pride for generations to come.

Bunyoro Kingdom

The Bunyoro Kingdom, also known as the Kingdom of Bunyoro-Kitara, was a prominent and influential civilization located in present-day Uganda, in East Africa. Flourishing from approximately the 16th century AD to the late 19th century AD, the Bunyoro Kingdom was one of the most significant states in the region, known for its political organization, military prowess, and cultural achievements. In this essay, we will delve into the history, economy, society, culture, governance, religion, architecture, and legacy of the Bunyoro Kingdom.

Origins and Early History:

The origins of the Bunyoro Kingdom can be traced back to the Bantu-speaking peoples who migrated into the region from the north and settled in the fertile lowlands of present-day Uganda. The Bunyoro people established a network of agricultural communities and trade routes, laying the foundations for the emergence of a centralized state. The rise of the Bunyoro Kingdom as a political entity coincided with the decline of earlier civilizations in the region, such as the Kingdom of Buganda.

Rise to Power:

The Bunyoro Kingdom reached its zenith during the 17th and 18th centuries when it became a major center of trade, culture, and political authority in East Africa. Under the leadership of its rulers, Bunyoro expanded its territory through conquest and alliance building, establishing a network of tributary states and client kingdoms. The kingdom's strategic location in the Nile River basin facilitated commerce and cultural exchange with neighboring civilizations, including the Kingdom of Buganda, the Kingdom of Rwanda, and Arab traders from the Swahili coast.

Economy and Trade:

The economy of the Bunyoro Kingdom was based primarily on agriculture, with the cultivation of crops such as millet, sorghum, maize, and bananas supporting a growing population. Bunyoro's access to fertile soil and reliable rainfall in the Nile region facilitated agriculture and allowed for the development of urban centers and settlements. Additionally, the kingdom controlled important trade routes linking East Africa with the Indian Ocean and the Swahili coast, enabling the exchange of goods such as ivory, copper, salt, slaves, and luxury items.

Society and Culture:

Bunyoro society was hierarchical, with a ruling class of kings, nobles, and warriors overseeing the administration of the kingdom. Below them were artisans, merchants, farmers, and laborers, while slaves performed menial tasks. The Bunyoro people were known for their artistic achievements, particularly in the fields of sculpture, pottery, and weaving. Bunyoro artisans created intricate works of art depicting human figures, animals, and geometric patterns, which served as symbols of royal power and cultural identity.

Governance and Administration:

The Bunyoro Kingdom was governed by a centralized monarchy, with power concentrated in the hands of the Omukama, or king. The Omukama ruled from the capital city of Mparo and exercised authority over a network of provincial governors, known as "Basiita." Local governance was facilitated by a system of tributary states and client kingdoms, which paid homage to the Omukama in exchange for protection and trade privileges. The kingdom's legal system was based on customary law and Bunyoro traditions, with councils and elders presiding over disputes and grievances.

Religion and Beliefs:

Religion played a central role in Bunyoro life, with the worship of a pantheon of gods and spirits representing various aspects of the natural world and human experience. The most important deity was Nyamata, the supreme god of the Bunyoro pantheon, who was venerated as the creator of the universe and the source of all life. Other important gods included the ancestors and spirits of nature. Bunyoro religious beliefs were expressed through rituals, ceremonies, and festivals honoring the gods and ancestors.

Decline and Legacy:

The decline of the Bunyoro Kingdom began in the late 19th century AD, as external pressures, internal conflicts, and the arrival of European colonial powers weakened its position. The kingdom's vulnerability was exploited by rival states, particularly the British, who sought to control the region's trade routes and resources. By the early 20th century AD, Bunyoro had been fragmented and weakened, eventually succumbing to conquest and colonization by European powers.

Despite its decline, the Bunyoro Kingdom left a lasting legacy that continues to shape the culture and history of Uganda and East Africa. Its political institutions, economic systems, and cultural traditions are a testament to the ingenuity, resilience, and enduring spirit of one of Africa's most remarkable civilizations. The legacy of the Bunyoro Kingdom lives on in the archaeological sites, artifacts, and oral traditions of the region, serving as a source of inspiration and pride for generations to come.

Buganda Kingdom

The Buganda Kingdom, also known as the Kingdom of Buganda, was a powerful and influential civilization located in present-day Uganda, in East Africa. Flourishing from approximately the 14th century AD to the late 19th century AD, the Buganda Kingdom was one of the most significant states in the region, known for its political organization, economic prosperity, and cultural achievements. In this essay, we will delve into the history, economy, society, culture, governance, religion, architecture, and legacy of the Buganda Kingdom.

• • • •

ORIGINS AND EARLY HISTORY:

The origins of the Buganda Kingdom can be traced back to the Bantu-speaking peoples who migrated into the region from the north and settled in the fertile lowlands of present-day Uganda. The Buganda people established a network of agricultural communities and trade routes, laying the foundations for the emergence of a centralized state. The rise of the Buganda Kingdom as a political entity coincided with the decline of earlier civilizations in the region.

Rise to Power:

The Buganda Kingdom reached its zenith during the 19th century when it became a major center of trade, culture, and political authority in East Africa. Under the leadership of its rulers, Buganda expanded its territory through conquest and alliance-building, establishing a network of tributary states and client kingdoms. The kingdom's strategic location in the Nile River basin facilitated commerce and cultural exchange with neighboring civilizations, including Bunyoro, Rwanda, and Arab traders from the Swahili coast.

Economy and Trade:

The economy of the Buganda Kingdom was based primarily on agriculture, with the cultivation of crops such as bananas, millet, sorghum, and sweet potatoes supporting a growing population. Buganda's access to fertile soil and reliable rainfall in the Nile region facilitated agriculture and allowed for the development of urban centers and settlements. Additionally, the kingdom controlled important trade routes linking East Africa with the Indian Ocean and the Swahili coast, enabling the exchange of goods such as ivory, copper, salt, slaves, and luxury items.

Society and Culture:

Buganda society was hierarchical, with a ruling class of kings, nobles, and chiefs overseeing the administration of the kingdom. Below them were artisans, merchants, farmers, and laborers, while slaves performed menial tasks. The Buganda people were known for their artistic achievements, particularly in the fields of music, dance, and literature. Buganda artists and musicians created intricate works of art and composed songs and poems that celebrated the kingdom's history, culture, and traditions.

Governance and Administration:

The Buganda Kingdom was governed by a centralized monarchy, with power concentrated in the hands of the Kabaka, or king. The Kabaka ruled from the capital city of Mengo and exercised authority over a network of provincial governors, known as "Bataka." Local governance was facilitated by a system of tributary states and client kingdoms, which paid homage to the Kabaka in exchange for protection and trade privileges. The kingdom's legal system was based on customary law and Buganda traditions, with councils and elders presiding over disputes and grievances.

Religion and Beliefs:

Religion played a central role in Buganda life, with the worship of a pantheon of gods and spirits representing various aspects of the natural world and human experience. The most important deity was Ggulu, the supreme god of the Buganda pantheon, who was venerated as the creator of the universe and the source of all life. Other important gods included the ancestors and spirits of nature. Buganda religious beliefs were expressed through rituals, ceremonies, and festivals honoring the gods and ancestors.

• • • •

DECLINE AND LEGACY:

The decline of the Buganda Kingdom began in the late 19th century AD, as external pressures, internal conflicts, and the arrival of European colonial powers weakened its position. The kingdom's vulnerability was exploited by rival states, particularly the British, who sought to control the region's trade routes and resources. By the early 20th century AD, Buganda had been fragmented and weakened, eventually succumbing to conquest and colonization by European powers.

Despite its decline, the Buganda Kingdom left a lasting legacy that continues to shape the culture and history of Uganda and East Africa. Its political institutions, economic systems, and cultural traditions are a testament to the ingenuity, resilience, and enduring spirit of one of Africa's most remarkable civilizations. The legacy of the Buganda Kingdom lives on in the archaeological sites, artifacts, and oral traditions of the region, serving as a source of inspiration and pride for generations to come.

Ankole Kingdom

The Ankole Kingdom, also known as the Kingdom of Ankole, was a prominent and influential civilization located in present-day Uganda, in East Africa. Flourishing from approximately the 15th century AD to the late 19th century AD, the Ankole Kingdom was one of the most significant states in the region, known for its distinct cultural practices, cattle-keeping economy, and elaborate governance system. In this essay, we will explore the history, economy, society, culture, governance, religion, architecture, and legacy of the Ankole Kingdom.

Origins and Early History:

The origins of the Ankole Kingdom can be traced back to the Bantu-speaking peoples who migrated into the region from the north and settled in the fertile grasslands of present-day Uganda. The Ankole people were primarily cattle herders, and their economy and culture revolved around the keeping of cattle. Over time, the Ankole established a centralized kingdom with a unique system of governance and social organization.

Rise to Power:

The Ankole Kingdom reached its zenith during the 18th and 19th centuries when it became a major center of cattle-keeping and trade in East Africa. Under the leadership of its rulers, Ankole expanded its territory through diplomacy and warfare, establishing alliances with neighboring kingdoms and chieftains. The kingdom's strategic location along trade routes facilitated commerce and cultural exchange with neighboring civilizations, including Buganda, Bunyoro, and Rwanda.

Economy and Trade:

The economy of the Ankole Kingdom was primarily based on cattle-keeping, with the Ankole people renowned for their large herds of long-horned cattle. Cattle were central to Ankole society, serving as a symbol of wealth, status, and power. The Ankole engaged in trade with neighboring kingdoms, exchanging cattle, hides, and other livestock products for agricultural produce, iron, salt, and luxury items. Trade routes crisscrossed the kingdom, connecting Ankole with the Indian Ocean coast and the interior of Africa.

Society and Culture:

Ankole society was organized into a hierarchical system with a ruling class of kings, chiefs, and elders at the top. Below them were commoners, including cattle herders, farmers, artisans, and laborers. The Ankole people had a rich cultural heritage, with elaborate rituals, ceremonies, and festivals celebrating important milestones such as marriage, childbirth, and harvest. Music, dance, and storytelling were integral parts of Ankole culture, with traditional songs and folk tales passed down through generations.

Governance and Administration:

The Ankole Kingdom was governed by a centralized monarchy, with power vested in the king, known as the Omugabe. The Omugabe ruled from the capital city of Nkore and exercised authority over a network of chiefs and clan leaders. Local governance was decentralized, with each clan or chiefdom responsible for the administration of its territory. Disputes were resolved through councils of elders, who served as mediators and arbitrators.

Religion and Beliefs:

Religion played a significant role in Ankole life, with the Ankole people adhering to a traditional belief system that centered around the worship of ancestral spirits and nature deities. The Ankole believed in the existence of a supreme being, known as Ruhanga, who created the universe and governed the forces of nature. Ancestral spirits were venerated as intermediaries between the living and the divine, with rituals and sacrifices performed to honor and appease them.

Decline and Legacy:

The decline of the Ankole Kingdom began in the late 19th century AD, with the arrival of European explorers and colonial powers. The kingdom's vulnerability was further exacerbated by internal conflicts and external pressures from neighboring kingdoms. Eventually, Ankole was absorbed into the British Protectorate of Uganda in the early 20th century, marking the end of its sovereignty as an independent kingdom.

Despite its decline, the Ankole Kingdom left a lasting legacy that continues to shape the culture and identity of the people of present-day Uganda. Its cattle-keeping traditions, cultural practices, and governance systems are still evident in Ankole society today. The kingdom's rich history and heritage are preserved in oral traditions, rituals, and ceremonies passed down through generations. The legacy of the Ankole Kingdom serves as a reminder of the resilience and ingenuity of one of East Africa's most remarkable civilizations.

Kingdom of Rwanda

The Kingdom of Rwanda, also known as the Rwandan Kingdom, was a significant and influential civilization located in present-day Rwanda, in East Africa. Flourishing from approximately the 15th century AD to the late 19th century AD, the Kingdom of Rwanda was known for its unique social structure, centralized governance, and rich cultural heritage. In this essay, we will explore the history, economy, society, culture, governance, religion, architecture, and legacy of the Kingdom of Rwanda.

Origins and Early History:

The origins of the Kingdom of Rwanda can be traced back to the Bantu-speaking peoples who migrated into the region from the north and settled in the hilly terrain of present-day Rwanda. The Rwandan people established a network of agricultural communities and trade routes, laying the foundations for the emergence of a centralized state. The rise of the Kingdom of Rwanda as a political entity coincided with the decline of earlier civilizations in the region.

Rise to Power:

The Kingdom of Rwanda reached its zenith during the 18th and 19th centuries when it became a major center of trade, culture, and political authority in East Africa. Under the leadership of its rulers, Rwanda expanded its territory through conquest and alliance-building, establishing a network of tributary states and client kingdoms. The kingdom's strategic location in the Great Lakes region facilitated commerce and cultural exchange with neighboring civilizations, including Buganda, Bunyoro, and Ankole.

Economy and Trade:

The economy of the Kingdom of Rwanda was based primarily on agriculture, with the cultivation of crops such as sorghum, beans, maize, and bananas supporting a growing population. Rwanda's rugged terrain and fertile soil facilitated agriculture and allowed for the development of terraced fields and irrigation systems. Additionally, the kingdom controlled important trade routes linking East Africa with the Indian Ocean coast, enabling the exchange of goods such as ivory, cattle, salt, and luxury items.

Society and Culture:

Rwandan society was characterized by a complex social structure based on kinship, lineage, and clan affiliation. At the top of the hierarchy was the Tutsi aristocracy, who held political and economic power, followed by the Hutu majority, who were primarily engaged in agriculture and livestock herding. Below them were the Twa, a marginalized minority group who were traditionally hunter-gatherers. Rwandan culture was rich and diverse, with elaborate rituals, ceremonies, and festivals celebrating important events such as birth, marriage, and death.

Governance and Administration:

The Kingdom of Rwanda was governed by a centralized monarchy, with power concentrated in the hands of the mwami, or king. The mwami ruled from the capital city of Nyanza and exercised authority over a network of chiefs and sub-chiefs. Local governance was decentralized, with each chiefdom responsible for the administration of its territory. Disputes were resolved through a system of customary law and traditional courts, presided over by elders and councilors.

Religion and Beliefs:

Religion played a central role in Rwandan life, with the Rwandan people adhering to a traditional belief system that centered around the worship of ancestral spirits and nature deities. The most important deity was Imana, the supreme god of the Rwandan pantheon, who was venerated as the creator of the universe and the source of all life. Ancestral spirits were revered as intermediaries between the living and the divine, with rituals and sacrifices performed to honor and appease them.

Decline and Legacy:

The decline of the Kingdom of Rwanda began in the late 19th century AD, as external pressures, internal conflicts, and the arrival of European colonial powers weakened its position. The kingdom's vulnerability was further exacerbated by the imposition of colonial rule and the introduction of Western political and economic systems. Eventually, Rwanda was absorbed into the German East Africa colony in the early 20th century, marking the end of its sovereignty as an independent kingdom.

Despite its decline, the Kingdom of Rwanda left a lasting legacy that continues to shape the culture and identity of the people of present-day Rwanda. Its social structure, governance systems, and cultural traditions are still evident in Rwandan society today. The kingdom's rich history and heritage are preserved in oral traditions, rituals, and ceremonies passed down through generations. The legacy of the Kingdom of Rwanda serves as a reminder of the resilience and ingenuity of one of East Africa's most remarkable civilizations.

Kingdom of Burundi

The Kingdom of Burundi, also known as the Kingdom of Urundi, was a significant and influential civilization located in present-day Burundi, in East Africa. Flourishing from approximately the 17th century AD to the late 19th century AD, the Kingdom of Burundi was known for its unique social structure, centralized governance, and rich cultural heritage. In this essay, we will explore the history, economy, society, culture, governance, religion, architecture, and legacy of the Kingdom of Burundi.

Origins and Early History:

The origins of the Kingdom of Burundi can be traced back to the Bantu-speaking peoples who migrated into the region from the north and settled in the fertile highlands of present-day Burundi. The Burundi people established a network of agricultural communities and trade routes, laying the foundations for the emergence of a centralized state. The rise of the Kingdom of Burundi as a political entity coincided with the decline of earlier civilizations in the region.

Rise to Power:

The Kingdom of Burundi reached its zenith during the 18th and 19th centuries when it became a major center of trade, culture, and political authority in East Africa. Under the leadership of its rulers, Burundi expanded its territory through conquest and alliance-building, establishing a network of tributary states and client kingdoms. The kingdom's strategic location in the Great Lakes region facilitated commerce and cultural exchange with neighboring civilizations, including Rwanda, Buganda, and Bunyoro.

Economy and Trade:

The economy of the Kingdom of Burundi was based primarily on agriculture, with the cultivation of crops such as sorghum, beans, maize, and bananas supporting a growing population. Burundi's fertile highlands and temperate climate facilitated agriculture and allowed for the development of terraced fields and irrigation systems. Additionally, the kingdom controlled important trade routes linking East Africa with the Indian Ocean coast, enabling the exchange of goods such as ivory, cattle, salt, and luxury items.

Society and Culture:

Burundi society was characterized by a complex social structure based on kinship, lineage, and clan affiliation. At the top of the hierarchy was the Tutsi aristocracy, who held political and economic power, followed by the Hutu majority, who were primarily engaged in agriculture and livestock herding. Below them were the Twa, a marginalized minority group who were traditionally hunter-gatherers. Burundi culture was rich and diverse, with elaborate rituals, ceremonies, and festivals celebrating important events such as birth, marriage, and death.

Governance and Administration:

The Kingdom of Burundi was governed by a centralized monarchy, with power concentrated in the hands of the mwami, or king. The mwami ruled from the capital city of Gitega and exercised authority over a network of chiefs and sub-chiefs. Local governance was decentralized, with each chiefdom responsible for the administration of its territory. Disputes were resolved through a system of customary law and traditional courts, presided over by elders and councilors.

Religion and Beliefs:

Religion played a central role in Burundi life, with the Burundi people adhering to a traditional belief system that centered around the worship of ancestral spirits and nature deities. The most important deity was Imana, the supreme god of the Burundi pantheon, who was venerated as the creator of the universe and the source of all life. Ancestral spirits were revered as intermediaries between the living and the divine, with rituals and sacrifices performed to honor and appease them.

• • • •

DECLINE AND LEGACY:

The decline of the Kingdom of Burundi began in the late 19th century AD, as external pressures, internal conflicts, and the arrival of European colonial powers weakened its position. The kingdom's vulnerability was further exacerbated by the imposition of colonial rule and the introduction of Western political and economic systems. Eventually, Burundi was absorbed into the German East Africa colony in the early 20th century, marking the end of its sovereignty as an independent kingdom.

Despite its decline, the Kingdom of Burundi left a lasting legacy that continues to shape the culture and identity of the people of present-day Burundi. Its social structure, governance systems, and cultural traditions are still evident in Burundi society today. The kingdom's rich history and heritage are preserved in oral traditions, rituals, and ceremonies passed down through generations. The legacy of the Kingdom of Burundi serves as a reminder of the resilience and ingenuity of one of East Africa's most remarkable civilizations.

The Swahili City-States were a network of independent urban settlements along the eastern coast of Africa, from present-day Somalia to Mozambique, which flourished from around the 9th to the 15th century AD. These city-states were known for their vibrant trade networks, diverse cultures, and distinctive architecture, reflecting the influence of Indian Ocean trade and interactions with various African, Arab, Persian, and Indian cultures. In this essay, we will explore the history, economy, society, culture, governance, religion, architecture, and legacy of the Swahili City-States.

Origins and Early History:

The origins of the Swahili City-States can be traced back to the early centuries AD when indigenous Bantu-speaking peoples established settlements along the East African coast. These communities engaged in fishing, farming, and trade with inland societies. Over time, these settlements grew into prosperous urban centers, fueled by the influx of traders from across the Indian Ocean and the Red Sea.

Rise to Power:

The Swahili City-States reached their zenith during the medieval period when they became major hubs of maritime trade between East Africa, the Arabian Peninsula, Persia, India, and China. The city-states flourished due to their strategic location along the Indian Ocean trade routes, which facilitated the exchange of goods such as gold, ivory, slaves, spices, textiles, porcelain, and precious metals.

Economy and Trade:

The economy of the Swahili City-States was centered around maritime trade, with merchants and traders conducting business in bustling port cities such as Mogadishu, Mombasa, Kilwa, Lamu, Malindi, and Zanzibar. Trade goods were transported by dhows, traditional wooden sailing vessels, which plied the waters of the Indian

Ocean. The Swahili traded with merchants from Arabia, Persia, India, and China, exchanging African products for luxury goods and commodities.

Society and Culture:

Swahili society was cosmopolitan and multicultural, with a diverse population consisting of indigenous Africans, Arab traders, Persian settlers, Indian merchants, and Chinese sailors. The Swahili people were known for their linguistic diversity, speaking various dialects of Swahili, a Bantu language enriched with Arabic, Persian, and Indian loanwords. Swahili culture was characterized by a blend of indigenous African, Islamic, and Asian influences, reflected in art, music, cuisine, and religious practices.

• • • •

GOVERNANCE AND ADMINISTRATION:

The Swahili City-States were governed by local rulers, known as sultans or sheikhs, who presided over urban centers and surrounding territories. These rulers derived their authority from a combination of local traditions, Islamic law, and commercial interests. Governance was often decentralized, with each city-state operating as an independent entity, although some city-states formed alliances or came under the influence of larger empires such as the Sultanate of Oman.

Religion and Beliefs:

Islam played a significant role in Swahili society, with the majority of the population adhering to Sunni Islam, which was introduced to the region by Arab and Persian traders and settlers. Mosques and madrasas, Islamic schools, were prominent features of Swahili urban centers, serving as centers of worship, education, and community life. Islamic beliefs and practices influenced various aspects of Swahili culture, including law, ethics, and social customs.

Architecture and Urban Planning:

Swahili architecture was characterized by its distinctive style, featuring coral stone buildings with ornate wooden doors, carved plasterwork, and domed rooftops. The most iconic architectural feature of the Swahili City-States was the stone townhouses, known as "Swahili houses," which featured courtyard gardens, verandas, and open-air terraces. Urban centers were organized around central squares or marketplaces, with narrow alleyways and winding streets connecting residential areas with commercial districts and waterfronts.

Decline and Legacy:

The decline of the Swahili City-States began in the late medieval period, as external pressures, including Portuguese and Omani incursions, disrupted trade networks and weakened urban centers. By the 16th century, many Swahili city-states had fallen under Portuguese or Omani control, marking the end of their independence as autonomous entities. However, the legacy of the Swahili City-States lives on in the cultural heritage, architectural legacy, and linguistic diversity of the East African coast. Swahili culture continues to thrive in coastal communities, serving as a testament to the enduring legacy of one of Africa's most vibrant and cosmopolitan civilizations.

Mombasa Sultanate

The Mombasa Sultanate was a significant and influential civilization located in present-day Kenya, on the East African coast. Flourishing from approximately the 9th to the 19th century AD, the Mombasa Sultanate was a key player in the Swahili Coast's trade network and cultural exchange, contributing to the region's rich history and heritage. In this essay, we will delve into the history, economy, society, culture, governance, religion, architecture, and legacy of the Mombasa Sultanate.

Origins and Early History:

The Mombasa Sultanate's origins can be traced back to the early centuries AD when indigenous Bantu-speaking peoples established settlements along the East African coast. Mombasa, strategically located on an island along the trade routes of the Indian Ocean, grew into a prosperous trading port. The influx of Arab and Persian traders, along with Indian and Chinese merchants, enriched the city's cultural landscape and facilitated the exchange of goods and ideas.

Rise to Power:

The Mombasa Sultanate reached its zenith during the medieval period when it became a major center of maritime trade between East Africa, the Arabian Peninsula, Persia, India, and China. Under the leadership of its sultans, Mombasa developed into a cosmopolitan city-state, attracting merchants, sailors, and scholars from across the Indian Ocean world. The sultanate flourished due to its strategic location and control over lucrative trade routes.

Economy and Trade:

The economy of the Mombasa Sultanate was centered around maritime trade, with merchants and traders conducting business in the bustling port city. Mombasa served as a hub for the exchange of goods such as gold, ivory, spices, textiles, porcelain, and precious metals. Trade was facilitated by the city's natural harbor and well-developed infrastructure, including warehouses, marketplaces, and docking facilities for dhows, traditional sailing vessels.

Society and Culture:

Mombasa society was cosmopolitan and multicultural, with a diverse population consisting of indigenous Africans, Arab and Persian traders, Indian merchants, and Chinese sailors. Swahili, a lingua franca derived from Bantu languages enriched with Arabic, Persian, and Indian loanwords, was spoken by the inhabitants of Mombasa. The city's cultural landscape was characterized by a blend of indigenous African, Islamic, and Asian influences, reflected in art, music, cuisine, and religious practices.

• • • •

GOVERNANCE AND ADMINISTRATION:

The Mombasa Sultanate was governed by local rulers, known as sultans, who presided over urban centers and surrounding territories. These rulers derived their authority from a combination of local traditions, Islamic law, and commercial interests. Governance was often decentralized, with each city-state operating as an independent entity, although some sultanates formed alliances or came under the influence of larger empires such as the Sultanate of Oman.

Religion and Beliefs:

Islam played a significant role in Mombasa society, with the majority of the population adhering to Sunni Islam. Mosques and madrasas, Islamic schools, were prominent features of Mombasa's urban landscape, serving as centers of worship, education, and community life. Islamic beliefs and practices influenced various aspects of Mombasa's culture, including law, ethics, and social customs.

Architecture and Urban Planning:

Mombasa's architecture was characterized by its distinctive style, featuring coral stone buildings with ornate wooden doors, carved plasterwork, and domed rooftops. The city's skyline was dominated by mosques, minarets, and fortifications, which served as symbols of Mombasa's prosperity and power. Urban centers were organized around central squares or marketplaces, with narrow alleyways and winding streets connecting residential areas with commercial districts and waterfronts.

Decline and Legacy:

The decline of the Mombasa Sultanate began in the late medieval period, as external pressures, including Portuguese and Omani incursions, disrupted trade networks and weakened urban centers. By the 19th century, Mombasa had fallen under Omani control, marking the end of its independence as an autonomous entity. However, the legacy of the Mombasa Sultanate lives on in the cultural heritage, architectural legacy, and maritime traditions of the East African coast. Mombasa continues to thrive as a vibrant and cosmopolitan city, serving as a testament to the enduring legacy of one of Africa's most remarkable civilizations.

Pate Sultanate

The Pate Sultanate was a significant and influential civilization located on the eastern coast of Africa, in present-day Kenya. Flourishing from approximately the 7th to the 19th century AD, the Pate Sultanate was renowned for its strategic location along the Indian Ocean trade routes and its vibrant cultural exchange with various African, Arab, Persian, and Indian civilizations. In this essay, we will delve into the history, economy, society, culture, governance, religion, architecture, and legacy of the Pate Sultanate.

Origins and Early History:

The origins of the Pate Sultanate can be traced back to the early centuries AD when indigenous Bantu-speaking peoples established settlements along the East African coast. Pate Island, located off the coast of present-day Kenya, served as the capital of the sultanate. The Pate Sultanate grew into a prosperous trading port, attracting merchants, sailors, and scholars from across the Indian Ocean world.

Rise to Power:

The Pate Sultanate reached its zenith during the medieval period when it became a major center of maritime trade between East Africa, the Arabian Peninsula, Persia, India, and China. Under the leadership of its sultans, Pate developed into a cosmopolitan city-state, known for its bustling markets, thriving economy, and vibrant cultural life. The sultanate flourished due to its control over lucrative trade routes and its strategic alliances with neighboring city-states.

Economy and Trade:

The economy of the Pate Sultanate was centered around maritime trade, with merchants and traders conducting business in the bustling port city of Pate. The sultanate served as a hub for the exchange of goods such as gold, ivory, spices, textiles, porcelain, and precious metals. Trade was facilitated by the city's natural harbor and well-developed infrastructure, including warehouses, marketplaces, and docking facilities for dhows, traditional sailing vessels.

Society and Culture:

Pate society was cosmopolitan and multicultural, with a diverse population consisting of indigenous Africans, Arab and Persian traders, Indian merchants, and Chinese sailors. Swahili, a lingua franca derived from Bantu languages enriched with Arabic, Persian, and Indian loanwords, was spoken by the inhabitants of Pate. The city's cultural landscape was characterized by a blend of indigenous African, Islamic, and Asian influences, reflected in art, music, cuisine, and religious practices.

· · · ·

GOVERNANCE AND ADMINISTRATION:

The Pate Sultanate was governed by local rulers, known as sultans, who presided over urban centers and surrounding territories. These rulers derived their authority from a combination of local traditions, Islamic law, and commercial interests. Governance was often decentralized, with each city-state operating as an independent entity, although some sultanates formed alliances or came under the influence of larger empires such as the Sultanate of Oman.

Religion and Beliefs:

Islam played a significant role in Pate society, with the majority of the population adhering to Sunni Islam. Mosques and madrasas, Islamic schools, were prominent features of Pate's urban landscape, serving as centers of worship, education, and community life. Islamic beliefs and practices influenced various aspects of Pate's culture, including law, ethics, and social customs.

Architecture and Urban Planning:

Pate's architecture was characterized by its distinctive style, featuring coral stone buildings with ornate wooden doors, carved plasterwork, and domed rooftops. The city's skyline was dominated by mosques, minarets, and fortifications, which served as symbols of Pate's prosperity and power. Urban centers were organized around central squares or marketplaces, with narrow alleyways and winding streets connecting residential areas with commercial districts and waterfronts.

Decline and Legacy:

The decline of the Pate Sultanate began in the late medieval period, as external pressures, including Portuguese and Omani incursions, disrupted trade networks and weakened urban centers. By the 19th century, Pate had fallen under Omani control, marking the end of its independence as an autonomous entity. However, the legacy of the Pate Sultanate lives on in the cultural heritage, architectural legacy, and maritime traditions of the East African coast. Pate continues to thrive as a vibrant and cosmopolitan city, serving as a testament to the enduring legacy of one of Africa's most remarkable civilizations.

Mogadishu Sultanate

The Mogadishu Sultanate, also known as the Sultanate of Mogadishu, was a significant civilization located on the eastern coast of Africa, in present-day Somalia. Flourishing from approximately the 10th to the 16th century AD, the Mogadishu Sultanate was renowned for its strategic location along the Indian Ocean trade routes and its vibrant cultural exchange with various African, Arab, Persian, and Indian civilizations. In this essay, we will explore the history, economy, society, culture, governance, religion, architecture, and legacy of the Mogadishu Sultanate.

Origins and Early History:

The origins of the Mogadishu Sultanate can be traced back to the early centuries AD when indigenous Cushitic-speaking peoples established settlements along the East African coast. Mogadishu, located on the Horn of Africa, grew into a prosperous trading port, attracting merchants, sailors, and scholars from across the Indian Ocean world. The sultanate benefited from its strategic location, which allowed it to control lucrative trade routes and engage in maritime commerce.

Rise to Power:

The Mogadishu Sultanate reached its zenith during the medieval period when it became a major center of maritime trade between East Africa, the Arabian Peninsula, Persia, India, and China. Under the leadership of its sultans, Mogadishu developed into a cosmopolitan city-state, known for its bustling markets, thriving economy, and vibrant cultural life. The sultanate flourished due to its control over lucrative trade routes and its strategic alliances with neighboring city-states.

Economy and Trade:

The economy of the Mogadishu Sultanate was centered around maritime trade, with merchants and traders conducting business in the bustling port city of Mogadishu. The sultanate served as a hub for the exchange of goods such as gold, ivory, spices, textiles, porcelain, and precious metals. Trade was facilitated by the city's natural harbor and well-developed infrastructure, including warehouses, marketplaces, and docking facilities for dhows, traditional sailing vessels.

Society and Culture:

Mogadishu society was cosmopolitan and multicultural, with a diverse population consisting of indigenous Cushitic-speaking peoples, Arab and Persian traders, Indian merchants, and Chinese sailors. Arabic, Persian, and Swahili were spoken by the inhabitants of Mogadishu, reflecting the city's cultural diversity and linguistic richness. Mogadishu's cultural landscape was characterized by a blend of indigenous African, Islamic, and Asian influences, reflected in art, music, cuisine, and religious practices.

Governance and Administration:

The Mogadishu Sultanate was governed by local rulers, known as sultans, who presided over urban centers and surrounding territories. These rulers derived their authority from a combination of local traditions, Islamic law, and commercial interests. Governance was often decentralized, with each city-state operating as an independent entity, although some sultanates formed alliances or came under the influence of larger empires such as the Sultanate of Oman.

Religion and Beliefs:

Islam played a significant role in Mogadishu society, with the majority of the population adhering to Sunni Islam. Mosques and madrasas, Islamic schools, were prominent features of Mogadishu's urban landscape, serving as centers of worship, education, and community life. Islamic beliefs and practices influenced various aspects of Mogadishu's culture, including law, ethics, and social customs.

Architecture and Urban Planning:

Mogadishu's architecture was characterized by its distinctive style, featuring coral stone buildings with ornate wooden doors, carved plasterwork, and domed rooftops. The city's skyline was dominated by mosques, minarets, and fortifications, which served as symbols of Mogadishu's prosperity and power. Urban centers were organized around central squares or marketplaces, with narrow alleyways and winding streets connecting residential areas with commercial districts and waterfronts.

Decline and Legacy:

The decline of the Mogadishu Sultanate began in the late medieval period, as external pressures, including Portuguese and Omani incursions, disrupted trade networks and weakened urban centers. By the 16th century, Mogadishu had fallen under Omani control, marking the end of its independence as an autonomous entity. However, the legacy of the Mogadishu Sultanate lives on in the cultural heritage, architectural legacy, and maritime traditions of the East African coast. Mogadishu continues to thrive as a vibrant and cosmopolitan city, serving as a testament to the enduring legacy of one of Africa's most remarkable civilizations.

Ajuran Sultanate

The Ajuran Sultanate was a powerful and influential civilization located in the Horn of Africa, in present-day Somalia. Flourishing from approximately the 13th to the 17th century AD, the Ajuran Sultanate was renowned for its military prowess, sophisticated administration, and significant contributions to Somali culture, society, and governance. In this essay, we will explore the history, economy, society, culture, governance, religion, architecture, and legacy of the Ajuran Sultanate.

Origins and Early History:

The origins of the Ajuran Sultanate can be traced back to the early medieval period when indigenous Cushitic-speaking peoples established settlements in the Horn of Africa. The Ajuran people, who hailed from the northern Somali region, rose to prominence as a dominant political and military force in the region. Through conquest and alliance-building, the Ajuran Sultanate expanded its territory and established control over key trade routes and urban centers.

Rise to Power:

The Ajuran Sultanate reached its zenith during the 14th and 15th centuries when it emerged as a major power in the Horn of Africa. Under the leadership of its sultans, the Ajuran Sultanate established a centralized state with a sophisticated administration and military organization. The sultanate flourished economically, politically, and culturally, attracting merchants, scholars, and artisans from across the Indian Ocean world.

Economy and Trade:

The economy of the Ajuran Sultanate was centered around agriculture, trade, and maritime commerce. The sultanate's fertile land and favorable climate supported the cultivation of crops such as sorghum, maize, millet, and sesame. Additionally, the Ajuran Sultanate controlled important trade routes linking the interior of Africa with the Indian Ocean coast, enabling the exchange of goods such as gold, ivory, slaves, spices, textiles, and precious metals.

Society and Culture:

Ajuran society was characterized by its rich cultural heritage, which reflected the diverse influences of indigenous Somali, Arab, Persian, and Indian cultures. Somali, a Cushitic language, served as the lingua franca of the Ajuran Sultanate, spoken by the majority of the population. The sultanate's cultural landscape was marked by a blend of Islamic, African, and Arab influences, evident in art, literature, music, cuisine, and religious practices.

Governance and Administration:

The Ajuran Sultanate was governed by a centralized monarchy, with power concentrated in the hands of the sultan and his council of advisors. The sultanate was divided into administrative regions, each governed by a provincial governor appointed by the sultan. The Ajuran Sultanate implemented a system of taxation, justice, and public works, including the construction of forts, mosques, and irrigation systems to support agriculture and infrastructure development.

Religion and Beliefs:

Islam played a central role in Ajuran society, with the majority of the population adhering to Sunni Islam. The sultanate's rulers and elites were patrons of Islamic scholarship, sponsoring the construction of mosques, madrasas, and religious institutions. Islamic law, ethics, and customs influenced various aspects of Ajuran life, including governance, education, and social organization.

Architecture and Urban Planning:

The Ajuran Sultanate was known for its impressive architectural achievements, including the construction of fortified settlements, mosques, and palaces. The sultanate's capital, Merca, was renowned for its well-planned urban layout, with streets, markets, and public spaces organized according to Islamic principles of urban design. Ajuran architecture was characterized by its use of locally sourced materials such as coral stone, limestone, and wood, with decorative elements inspired by Islamic art and design.

Decline and Legacy:

The decline of the Ajuran Sultanate began in the late 16th century, as external pressures, including Portuguese and Ottoman incursions, disrupted trade networks and weakened the sultanate's authority. By the early 17th century, the Ajuran Sultanate had fragmented into smaller states, marking the end of its political dominance in the region. However, the legacy of the Ajuran Sultanate lives on in the cultural heritage, linguistic legacy, and historical memory of the Somali people. The sultanate's contributions to Somali culture, governance, and identity continue to be celebrated and remembered, serving as a testament to the enduring legacy of one of Africa's most remarkable civilizations.

The Adal Sultanate, also known as the Adal Kingdom, was a significant civilization located in the Horn of Africa, in present-day Somalia and parts of Ethiopia. Flourishing from approximately the 13th to the 17th century AD, the Adal Sultanate was renowned for its military prowess, cultural achievements, and contributions to the history of the region. In this essay, we will explore the history, economy, society, culture, governance, religion, architecture, and legacy of the Adal Sultanate.

· · · ·

ORIGINS AND EARLY HISTORY:

The origins of the Adal Sultanate can be traced back to the 13th century AD when indigenous Somali and Cushitic-speaking peoples established settlements in the Horn of Africa. The Sultanate emerged as a powerful state in the region, with its capital at Zeila, strategically located on the coast of the Gulf of Aden. Through conquest and alliance-building, the Adal Sultanate expanded its territory and exerted influence over neighboring city-states and kingdoms.

Rise to Power:

The Adal Sultanate reached its zenith during the 14th and 15th centuries when it emerged as a major power in the Horn of Africa. Under the leadership of its sultans, the Adal Sultanate established a centralized state with a sophisticated military organization and administrative apparatus. The sultanate flourished economically, politically, and culturally, attracting merchants, scholars, and artisans from across the Indian Ocean world.

Economy and Trade:

The economy of the Adal Sultanate was centered around agriculture, trade, and maritime commerce. The sultanate's fertile land

and favorable climate supported the cultivation of crops such as sorghum, maize, millet, and sesame. Additionally, the Adal Sultanate controlled important trade routes linking the interior of Africa with the Indian Ocean coast, enabling the exchange of goods such as gold, ivory, spices, textiles, and precious metals.

Society and Culture:

Adal society was characterized by its rich cultural heritage, which reflected the diverse influences of indigenous Somali, Arab, Persian, and Indian cultures. Somali, a Cushitic language, served as the lingua franca of the Adal Sultanate, spoken by the majority of the population. The sultanate's cultural landscape was marked by a blend of Islamic, African, and Arab influences, evident in art, literature, music, cuisine, and religious practices.

• • • •

GOVERNANCE AND ADMINISTRATION:

The Adal Sultanate was governed by a centralized monarchy, with power concentrated in the hands of the sultan and his council of advisors. The sultanate was divided into administrative regions, each governed by a provincial governor appointed by the sultan. The Adal Sultanate implemented a system of taxation, justice, and public works, including the construction of forts, mosques, and irrigation systems to support agriculture and infrastructure development.

Religion and Beliefs:

Islam played a central role in Adal society, with the majority of the population adhering to Sunni Islam. The sultanate's rulers and elites were patrons of Islamic scholarship, sponsoring the construction of mosques, madrasas, and religious institutions. Islamic law, ethics, and customs influenced various aspects of Adal life, including governance, education, and social organization.

Architecture and Urban Planning:

The Adal Sultanate was known for its impressive architectural achievements, including the construction of fortified settlements, mosques, and palaces. The sultanate's capital, Zeila, was renowned for its well-planned urban layout, with streets, markets, and public spaces organized according to Islamic principles of urban design. Adal architecture was characterized by its use of locally sourced materials such as coral stone, limestone, and wood, with decorative elements inspired by Islamic art and design.

Decline and Legacy:

The decline of the Adal Sultanate began in the late 16th century, as external pressures, including Portuguese and Ethiopian incursions, disrupted trade networks and weakened the sultanate's authority. By the early 17th century, the Adal Sultanate had fragmented into smaller states, marking the end of its political dominance in the region. However, the legacy of the Adal Sultanate lives on in the cultural heritage, linguistic legacy, and historical memory of the Somali people. The sultanate's contributions to Somali culture, governance, and identity continue to be celebrated and remembered, serving as a testament to the enduring legacy of one of Africa's most remarkable civilizations.

Ifat Sultanate

The Ifat Sultanate, also known as the Ifat Emirate, was a significant civilization located in the Horn of Africa, in present-day Ethiopia and parts of Somalia. Flourishing from approximately the 13th to the 15th century AD, the Ifat Sultanate played a crucial role in the region's political, economic, and cultural landscape. In this essay, we will explore the history, economy, society, culture, governance, religion, architecture, and legacy of the Ifat Sultanate.

Origins and Early History:

The origins of the Ifat Sultanate can be traced back to the 13th century AD when indigenous Somali and Cushitic-speaking peoples established settlements in the Horn of Africa. The Sultanate emerged as a powerful state in the region, with its capital at Zeila, strategically located on the coast of the Gulf of Aden. Through conquest and alliance-building, the Ifat Sultanate expanded its territory and exerted influence over neighboring city-states and kingdoms.

Rise to Power:

The Ifat Sultanate reached its zenith during the 14th and 15th centuries when it emerged as a major power in the Horn of Africa. Under the leadership of its sultans, the Ifat Sultanate established a centralized state with a sophisticated military organization and administrative apparatus. The sultanate flourished economically, politically, and culturally, attracting merchants, scholars, and artisans from across the Indian Ocean world.

Economy and Trade:

The economy of the Ifat Sultanate was centered around agriculture, trade, and maritime commerce. The sultanate's fertile land and favorable climate supported the cultivation of crops such as sorghum, maize, millet, and sesame. Additionally, the Ifat Sultanate controlled important trade routes linking the interior of Africa with the Indian

Ocean coast, enabling the exchange of goods such as gold, ivory, spices, textiles, and precious metals.

Society and Culture:

Ifat society was characterized by its rich cultural heritage, which reflected the diverse influences of indigenous Somali, Arab, Persian, and Indian cultures. Somali, a Cushitic language, served as the lingua franca of the Ifat Sultanate, spoken by the majority of the population. The sultanate's cultural landscape was marked by a blend of Islamic, African, and Arab influences, evident in art, literature, music, cuisine, and religious practices.

Governance and Administration:

The Ifat Sultanate was governed by a centralized monarchy, with power concentrated in the hands of the sultan and his council of advisors. The sultanate was divided into administrative regions, each governed by a provincial governor appointed by the sultan. The Ifat Sultanate implemented a system of taxation, justice, and public works, including the construction of forts, mosques, and irrigation systems to support agriculture and infrastructure development.

Religion and Beliefs:

Islam played a central role in Ifat society, with the majority of the population adhering to Sunni Islam. The sultanate's rulers and elites were patrons of Islamic scholarship, sponsoring the construction of mosques, madrasas, and religious institutions. Islamic law, ethics, and customs influenced various aspects of Ifat life, including governance, education, and social organization.

Architecture and Urban Planning:

The Ifat Sultanate was known for its impressive architectural achievements, including the construction of fortified settlements, mosques, and palaces. The sultanate's capital, Zeila, was renowned for its well-planned urban layout, with streets, markets, and public spaces organized according to Islamic principles of urban design. Ifat architecture was characterized by its use of locally sourced materials such as coral stone, limestone, and wood, with decorative elements inspired by Islamic art and design.

Decline and Legacy:

The decline of the Ifat Sultanate began in the late 15th century, as external pressures, including Ethiopian and Portuguese incursions, disrupted trade networks and weakened the sultanate's authority. By the early 16th century, the Ifat Sultanate had fragmented into smaller states, marking the end of its political dominance in the region. However, the legacy of the Ifat Sultanate lives on in the cultural heritage, linguistic legacy, and historical memory of the Somali people. The sultanate's contributions to Somali culture, governance, and identity continue to be celebrated and remembered, serving as a testament to the enduring legacy of one of Africa's most remarkable civilizations.

Harar Sultanate

The Harar Sultanate, also known as the Emirate of Harar, was a significant civilization located in the Horn of Africa, in present-day Ethiopia. Flourishing from approximately the 10th to the 19th century AD, the Harar Sultanate was renowned for its strategic location along trade routes, its vibrant cultural exchange, and its rich Islamic heritage. In this essay, we will explore the history, economy, society, culture, governance, religion, architecture, and legacy of the Harar Sultanate.

Origins and Early History:

The origins of the Harar Sultanate can be traced back to the early medieval period when indigenous peoples inhabited the region surrounding the city of Harar. Harar's strategic location along trade routes linking the Horn of Africa with the Arabian Peninsula and beyond contributed to its early development as a commercial and cultural center. Over time, Harar grew into a prosperous city-state, attracting merchants, scholars, and travelers from across the Indian Ocean world.

Rise to Power:

The Harar Sultanate reached its zenith during the 16th and 17th centuries when it emerged as a major power in the Horn of Africa. Under the leadership of its sultans, Harar became a center of Islamic scholarship, attracting renowned scholars and theologians. The sultanate flourished economically, politically, and culturally, with its influence extending throughout the region. Harar's strategic location made it a coveted prize for neighboring states and empires seeking to control trade routes and access to the Red Sea.

Economy and Trade:

The economy of the Harar Sultanate was centered around agriculture, trade, and commerce. The fertile land surrounding Harar supported the cultivation of crops such as grains, coffee, and qat, a stimulant plant popular in the region. Harar's location along trade routes facilitated the exchange of goods such as spices, textiles, ivory, and precious metals. The city's bustling markets attracted merchants from distant lands, contributing to its prosperity and cosmopolitan atmosphere.

Society and Culture:

Harar society was characterized by its rich cultural heritage, which reflected the diverse influences of indigenous African, Arab, and Islamic traditions. Arabic, a language of scholarship and religion, was widely spoken in Harar, alongside local languages such as Oromo and Somali. Harar's cultural landscape was marked by a blend of Islamic architecture, music, literature, and cuisine, creating a unique and vibrant cultural identity.

Governance and Administration:

The Harar Sultanate was governed by a centralized monarchy, with power vested in the sultan and his court. The sultanate's administrative structure included provincial governors, judges, and officials responsible for taxation, justice, and public works. Harar's rulers were patrons of Islamic art and scholarship, sponsoring the construction of mosques, madrasas, and other religious and educational institutions.

Religion and Beliefs:

Islam played a central role in Harar society, with the majority of the population adhering to Sunni Islam. Mosques and shrines dedicated to Islamic saints were prominent features of Harar's urban landscape, serving as centers of worship, education, and community life. Islamic law and ethics governed various aspects of daily life, including social customs, commerce, and governance.

Architecture and Urban Planning:

Harar's architecture was characterized by its distinctive style, featuring narrow winding streets, whitewashed buildings, and traditional courtyard houses. The city's skyline was punctuated by minarets, domes, and fortifications, which served as symbols of Harar's

Islamic identity and defensive strength. Harar's urban layout reflected Islamic principles of urban planning, with mosques, markets, and residential areas organized around central squares and courtyards.

Decline and Legacy:

The decline of the Harar Sultanate began in the 19th century, as external pressures, including European colonization and the expansion of Ethiopian rule, challenged its sovereignty. In 1875, Harar was annexed by Ethiopia, marking the end of its independence as an autonomous entity. However, the legacy of the Harar Sultanate lives on in the cultural heritage, architectural legacy, and historical memory of the region. Harar continues to be celebrated for its vibrant Islamic culture, rich history, and unique urban landscape, serving as a testament to the enduring legacy of one of Africa's most remarkable civilizations.

Mossi Kingdoms

The Mossi Kingdoms, also known as the Mossi States, were a group of independent kingdoms located in present-day Burkina Faso, West Africa. The Mossi people are a diverse ethnic group, consisting of several subgroups, each with its own distinct language, culture, and traditions. The Mossi Kingdoms emerged around the 11th century AD and played a significant role in shaping the political, social, and cultural landscape of the region. In this essay, we will explore the history, economy, society, culture, governance, religion, architecture, and legacy of the Mossi Kingdoms.

Origins and Early History:

The origins of the Mossi Kingdoms can be traced back to the migration of the Mossi people from the region of modern-day Ghana to the savannah lands of present-day Burkina Faso. The Mossi settled in the region and established a network of independent chiefdoms, each ruled by a local ruler known as a "moro naba." Over time, these chiefdoms coalesced into larger kingdoms, forming the foundation of the Mossi political structure.

Rise to Power:

The Mossi Kingdoms reached their zenith during the 15th and 16th centuries when they emerged as major powers in West Africa. Under the leadership of powerful rulers such as Naaba Zougrana and Naaba Ouedraogo, the Mossi Kingdoms expanded their territories through conquest and alliances, establishing control over vast swathes of land and trade routes. The Mossi became known for their military prowess, organizational skills, and administrative efficiency.

Economy and Trade:

The economy of the Mossi Kingdoms was primarily agrarian, with farming being the mainstay of the economy. The Mossi people cultivated crops such as millet, sorghum, maize, and rice, using sophisticated irrigation techniques to maximize agricultural output.

Trade also played a significant role in the Mossi economy, with the kingdoms serving as important intermediaries in the trans-Saharan trade network, facilitating the exchange of goods such as gold, salt, ivory, and slaves.

Society and Culture:

Mossi society was hierarchical, with a ruling elite known as the "moro naba" and a system of nobility, commoners, and slaves. Social status was determined by birth, with the ruling class enjoying privileges such as landownership, political power, and access to education. Mossi culture was characterized by its rich oral traditions, music, dance, and art, which played a central role in community life and identity.

Governance and Administration:

The Mossi Kingdoms were governed by a centralized monarchy, with power vested in the "moro naba" or king. The king was advised by a council of elders and officials responsible for administration, justice, and defense. Each kingdom was divided into administrative regions, each governed by a provincial chief appointed by the king. The Mossi kingdoms had well-developed systems of taxation, justice, and public works, including the construction of roads, bridges, and fortifications.

Religion and Beliefs:

The Mossi people practiced a traditional animist religion, worshipping ancestral spirits, natural forces, and supernatural beings. The "moro naba" served as the spiritual and political leader of the kingdom, acting as a mediator between the people and the spirit world. Islam and Christianity also made inroads into Mossi society, particularly during the colonial period, but traditional beliefs remained strong among the majority of the population.

Architecture and Urban Planning:

Mossi architecture was characterized by its use of locally available materials such as mud brick, thatch, and wood. The kingdoms were dotted with fortified settlements, known as "tata" or "somba," which served as centers of administration, defense, and commerce. The capitals of the Mossi Kingdoms were organized around central squares, marketplaces, and royal palaces, with narrow winding streets connecting different districts.

Decline and Legacy:

The decline of the Mossi Kingdoms began in the late 19th century with the arrival of European colonial powers, particularly the French. The Mossi Kingdoms were eventually incorporated into the French colonial empire, marking the end of their sovereignty as independent states. However, the legacy of the Mossi Kingdoms lives on in the cultural heritage, traditions, and collective memory of the Mossi people. The kingdoms' contributions to West African history, governance, and culture continue to be celebrated and remembered, serving as a source of pride and identity for generations to come.

The Mandinka Empire, also known as the Manding Empire or Mali Empire, was one of the most powerful and influential civilizations in West Africa, flourishing from approximately the 13th to the 17th century AD. Centered around the region of present-day Mali and extending into parts of Senegal, Guinea, Gambia, and Burkina Faso, the Mandinka Empire played a pivotal role in shaping the political, economic, and cultural landscape of the region. In this essay, we will explore the history, economy, society, culture, governance, religion, architecture, and legacy of the Mandinka Empire.

Origins and Early History:

The Mandinka Empire traces its origins to the ancient Mandinka people, who inhabited the region of West Africa known as the Manding plateau. The Mandinka were part of the larger Mande ethnic group, which also included the Soninke, Bambara, and Malinke peoples. The Mandinka established a network of independent chiefdoms and city-states, each ruled by a local leader known as a "mansa" or "king."

Rise to Power:

The Mandinka Empire reached its zenith during the 13th and 14th centuries under the leadership of Sundiata Keita, the founder of the Mali Empire. Sundiata united the disparate Mandinka chiefdoms and city-states under his rule, establishing a centralized state with its capital at Niani. Under Sundiata and his successors, the Mali Empire expanded rapidly, conquering neighboring states and kingdoms and establishing control over lucrative trade routes.

Economy and Trade:

The economy of the Mali Empire was based primarily on agriculture, with the cultivation of crops such as millet, sorghum, rice, and cotton forming the backbone of the economy. The empire also benefited from its control over important trade routes, including the trans-Saharan trade route, which facilitated the exchange of goods such as gold, salt, ivory, and slaves. Mali's wealth and prosperity attracted merchants, scholars, and travelers from across the Muslim world.

Society and Culture:

Mali society was characterized by its rich cultural heritage, which reflected the diverse influences of the Mandinka, Soninke, and other ethnic groups. The empire was home to various ethnic and religious communities, including Muslims, animists, and Christians, who coexisted and interacted within its borders. Mali's cultural landscape was marked by its oral traditions, music, dance, and art, which played a central role in community life and identity.

Governance and Administration:

The Mali Empire was governed by a centralized monarchy, with power vested in the "mansa" or king. The king was advised by a council of elders and officials responsible for administration, justice, and defense. Mali was divided into administrative regions, each governed by appointed officials responsible for taxation, justice, and public works. The empire had well-developed systems of governance, including a complex bureaucracy, legal code, and military organization.

Religion and Beliefs:

Islam played a central role in Mali society, with the majority of the population adhering to Sunni Islam. The "mansa" served as both the political and spiritual leader of the empire, acting as a mediator between the people and the divine. Islam influenced various aspects of Mali life, including governance, education, and social customs, but traditional beliefs and practices also persisted among certain segments of the population.

Architecture and Urban Planning:

Mali's architecture was characterized by its use of locally available materials such as mud brick, thatch, and wood. The empire was dotted with fortified settlements, royal palaces, mosques, and religious shrines, which served as centers of administration, defense, and worship. Mali's capital city, Niani, was renowned for its grandeur and splendor, with impressive architecture and urban planning reflecting the empire's wealth and power.

• • • •

DECLINE AND LEGACY:

The decline of the Mali Empire began in the late 16th century, as internal strife, external pressures, and dynastic conflicts weakened its authority. The empire eventually fragmented into smaller states and kingdoms, marking the end of its political dominance in the region. However, the legacy of the Mali Empire lives on in the cultural heritage, traditions, and collective memory of the Mandinka and other West African peoples. Mali's contributions to trade, scholarship, and governance continue to be celebrated and remembered, serving as a source of inspiration and pride for generations to come.

The Wadai Empire, also known as the Wadai Sultanate, was a powerful and influential civilization located in present-day Chad, Central Africa. Flourishing from the 16th to the 19th century AD, the Wadai Empire played a significant role in shaping the political, economic, and cultural landscape of the region. In this essay, we will explore the history, economy, society, culture, governance, religion, architecture, and legacy of the Wadai Empire.

Origins and Early History:

The origins of the Wadai Empire can be traced back to the medieval period when indigenous peoples inhabited the region of Wadai, located in the eastern part of present-day Chad. The area was characterized by its fertile land, abundant water sources, and strategic location along trade routes linking North Africa with sub-Saharan Africa. Over time, Wadai emerged as a center of commerce, attracting merchants, traders, and settlers from neighboring regions.

Rise to Power:

The Wadai Empire reached its zenith during the 17th and 18th centuries under the leadership of its greatest ruler, Muhammad Sabun. Muhammad Sabun united the disparate tribes and clans of Wadai under his rule, establishing a centralized state with its capital at Ouara. Under his leadership, Wadai expanded its territories through military conquest, bringing neighboring states and kingdoms under its control. The empire became known for its military prowess, organizational skills, and administrative efficiency.

Economy and Trade:

The economy of the Wadai Empire was primarily agrarian, with agriculture forming the backbone of the economy. The fertile land surrounding Wadai supported the cultivation of crops such as millet, sorghum, maize, and rice, which served as staple foods for the population. Wadai also benefited from its control over important trade routes, including the trans-Saharan trade route, which facilitated the exchange of goods such as gold, ivory, slaves, and salt.

Society and Culture:

Wadai society was characterized by its rich cultural diversity, with a mix of indigenous African, Arab, and Islamic influences. The empire was home to various ethnic groups, including the Maba, Daza, and Fulani peoples, who coexisted and intermingled within its borders. Islam played a central role in Wadai's cultural and religious life, shaping its customs, traditions, and social norms. The empire's cosmopolitan cities were centers of learning, trade, and artistic expression, fostering a vibrant cultural scene.

• • • •

GOVERNANCE AND ADMINISTRATION:

The Wadai Empire was governed by a centralized monarchy, with power vested in the sultan and his council of advisors. The empire was divided into administrative regions, each governed by appointed officials responsible for taxation, justice, and public works. Wadai's rulers were patrons of Islamic scholarship and culture, sponsoring the construction of mosques, madrasas, and other religious and educational institutions.

Religion and Beliefs:

Islam was the dominant religion in the Wadai Empire, with the majority of the population adhering to Sunni Islam. Mosques, Quranic schools, and religious shrines were prominent features of Wadai's urban landscape, serving as centers of worship, education, and community life. Islamic law and ethics governed various aspects of daily life, including governance, commerce, and social relations.

Architecture and Urban Planning:

Wadai's architecture was characterized by its use of locally available materials such as mud brick, thatch, and wood. The empire was dotted with fortified settlements, royal palaces, mosques, and religious shrines, which served as centers of administration, defense, and worship. Wadai's capital city, Ouara, was renowned for its grandeur and splendor, with impressive architecture and urban planning reflecting the empire's wealth and power.

Decline and Legacy:

The decline of the Wadai Empire began in the 19th century with the arrival of European colonial powers, particularly the French. Wadai was eventually incorporated into the French colonial empire, marking the end of its sovereignty as an independent state. However, the legacy of the Wadai Empire lives on in the cultural heritage, traditions, and collective memory of the people of Chad. The empire's contributions to trade, scholarship, and governance continue to be celebrated and remembered, serving as a source of inspiration and pride for generations to come.

Kingdom of Fouta Djallon

The Kingdom of Fouta Djallon, also known as the Fula Empire, was a significant pre-colonial state in West Africa, situated in the Fouta Djallon highlands of present-day Guinea and parts of Senegal, Mali, and Guinea-Bissau. Flourishing from the 18th to the 19th century, Fouta Djallon played a crucial role in the history and culture of the Fula people, who are primarily known for their pastoralist lifestyle and Islamic heritage. In this essay, we will delve into the history, economy, society, culture, governance, religion, architecture, and legacy of the Kingdom of Fouta Djallon.

Origins and Early History:

The Kingdom of Fouta Djallon traces its origins to the migration of Fula (also known as Fulani or Peul) pastoralists into the Fouta Djallon region in the 15th century. Over time, the Fula people established a network of pastoral settlements and engaged in trade, agriculture, and Islamic scholarship. By the 18th century, Fouta Djallon had emerged as a centralized state, with its capital at Timbo, ruled by a council of elders known as the "Almamis."

Rise to Power:

Fouta Djallon reached its zenith during the 18th and 19th centuries under the leadership of Alfa Ibrahima Sory Diallo, commonly known as Karamokho Alfa. Karamokho Alfa unified the disparate Fula clans and tribes of Fouta Djallon under his rule, establishing a centralized state with a sophisticated administrative system and a strict adherence to Islamic law and principles. Under his leadership, Fouta Djallon became a major center of Islamic learning, trade, and political power in West Africa.

Economy and Trade:

The economy of Fouta Djallon was primarily based on agriculture, with the cultivation of crops such as millet, sorghum, maize, and rice being the mainstay of the economy. The region's fertile soil and abundant water sources supported intensive agriculture, allowing Fouta Djallon to become largely self-sufficient in food production. Trade also played a significant role in the economy, with Fouta Djallon serving as a hub for the exchange of goods such as livestock, salt, cloth, and handicrafts.

Society and Culture:

Fouta Djallon society was characterized by its rich cultural heritage, which blended traditional Fula customs and Islamic beliefs. The Fula people practiced a pastoralist lifestyle, herding cattle, sheep, and goats across the region's grasslands and savannas. Islamic scholarship and education were highly valued in Fouta Djallon, with the region becoming renowned for its Quranic schools, mosques, and centers of learning. The Fula language, known as Pulaar or Fulfulde, was widely spoken, along with Arabic for religious and scholarly purposes.

Governance and Administration:

Fouta Djallon was governed by a centralized monarchy, with power vested in the "Almami" or ruler, who was advised by a council of elders and officials. The Almami's authority was based on a combination of Islamic law and traditional Fula customs, with justice administered through Sharia courts and customary law. The kingdom was divided into administrative districts, each governed by appointed officials responsible for taxation, justice, and public works.

Religion and Beliefs:

Islam played a central role in the life and culture of Fouta Djallon, with the majority of the population adhering to Sunni Islam. The Fula people embraced Islam during the 18th century, following the teachings of Muslim scholars and missionaries who spread the faith across West Africa. Islamic rituals, prayers, and festivals became integral parts of Fouta Djallon's cultural identity, shaping its social customs, moral values, and legal practices.

Architecture and Urban Planning:

Fouta Djallon's architecture was characterized by its traditional Fula-style houses, known as "round huts" or "cases," constructed from locally sourced materials such as mud, thatch, and wood. The kingdom's urban centers were organized around central squares, marketplaces, and mosques, with narrow winding streets connecting different districts. Mosques and Islamic schools served as focal points of community life, education, and worship, reflecting the region's strong Islamic heritage.

Decline and Legacy:

The Kingdom of Fouta Djallon began to decline in the 19th century due to internal strife, external pressures, and the encroachment of European colonial powers. The kingdom eventually fell to French colonial forces in the late 19th century, marking the end of its sovereignty as an independent state. However, the legacy of Fouta Djallon lives on in the cultural heritage, traditions, and collective memory of the Fula people. The kingdom's contributions to Islamic scholarship, pastoralism, and political organization continue to be celebrated and remembered, serving as a source of pride and identity for Fula communities across West Africa.

The Kingdom of Sine, also known as the Kingdom of Siin, was a pre-colonial state located in present-day Senegal, in the westernmost region of West Africa. Flourishing from the 14th to the 19th century AD, Sine played a significant role in the history and culture of the Wolof people, who are primarily known for their agricultural practices, trade networks, and Islamic heritage. In this essay, we will explore the history, economy, society, culture, governance, religion, architecture, and legacy of the Kingdom of Sine.

Origins and Early History:

The Kingdom of Sine traces its origins to the medieval period when the Wolof people migrated to the Senegambia region from the south and settled along the banks of the Senegal River. The Wolof established settlements and engaged in agriculture, fishing, and trade, building a network of villages and towns along the river valley. Over time, these settlements coalesced into a centralized state known as Sine, with its capital at Diakhao.

Rise to Power:

Sine reached its zenith during the 15th and 16th centuries under the leadership of its greatest ruler, Maad a Sinig Maysa Wali Jaxateh Manneh, commonly known as Maad a Sinig Maysa Wali. Maysa Wali unified the disparate Wolof clans and tribes of Sine under his rule, establishing a centralized state with a sophisticated administrative system and a strict adherence to Islamic law and principles. Under his leadership, Sine became a major center of trade, agriculture, and political power in the Senegambia region.

Economy and Trade:

The economy of Sine was primarily based on agriculture, with the cultivation of crops such as millet, sorghum, rice, and groundnuts forming the backbone of the economy. The region's fertile soil and abundant water sources supported intensive agriculture, allowing Sine to become largely self-sufficient in food production. Trade also played a significant role in the economy, with Sine serving as a hub for the exchange of goods such as salt, cloth, cattle, and slaves.

Society and Culture:

Sine society was characterized by its rich cultural heritage, which blended traditional Wolof customs and Islamic beliefs. The Wolof people practiced a predominantly agricultural lifestyle, cultivating crops, raising livestock, and fishing in the rivers and lakes of the region. Islamic education and scholarship were highly valued in Sine, with Quranic schools, mosques, and Islamic scholars playing important roles in the community. The Wolof language, known as Wolof, was widely spoken, along with Arabic for religious and scholarly purposes.

• • • •

GOVERNANCE AND ADMINISTRATION:

Sine was governed by a centralized monarchy, with power vested in the Maad a Sinig or king, who was advised by a council of elders and officials. The Maad a Sinig's authority was based on a combination of traditional Wolof customs and Islamic law, with justice administered through Sharia courts and customary law. The kingdom was divided into administrative districts, each governed by appointed officials responsible for taxation, justice, and public works.

Religion and Beliefs:

Islam played a central role in the life and culture of Sine, with the majority of the population adhering to Sunni Islam. The Wolof people embraced Islam during the 15th and 16th centuries, following the teachings of Muslim scholars and missionaries who spread the faith across the Senegambia region. Islamic rituals, prayers, and festivals became integral parts of Sine's cultural identity, shaping its social customs, moral values, and legal practices.

Architecture and Urban Planning:

Sine's architecture was characterized by its traditional Wolof-style houses, constructed from locally sourced materials such as mud, thatch, and wood. The kingdom's urban centers were organized around central squares, marketplaces, and mosques, with narrow winding streets connecting different districts. Mosques and Quranic schools served as focal points of community life, education, and worship, reflecting the region's strong Islamic heritage.

Decline and Legacy:

The Kingdom of Sine began to decline in the 19th century due to internal strife, external pressures, and the encroachment of European colonial powers. The kingdom eventually fell to French colonial forces in the late 19th century, marking the end of its sovereignty as an independent state. However, the legacy of Sine lives on in the cultural heritage, traditions, and collective memory of the Wolof people. The kingdom's contributions to agriculture, trade, and Islamic scholarship continue to be celebrated and remembered, serving as a source of pride and identity for Wolof communities in Senegal and beyond.

Kingdom of Saloum

The Kingdom of Saloum, also known as the Salum or Saluum, was a pre-colonial state situated in present-day Senegal, West Africa. Flourishing from the 15th to the 19th century, Saloum played a significant role in the history and culture of the Serer people, who are primarily known for their agricultural practices, social organization, and religious traditions. In this essay, we will delve into the history, economy, society, culture, governance, religion, architecture, and legacy of the Kingdom of Saloum.

Origins and Early History:

The Kingdom of Saloum traces its origins to the medieval period when the Serer people migrated to the Senegambia region and settled along the banks of the Saloum River. The Serer established settlements and engaged in agriculture, fishing, and trade, building a network of villages and towns along the river valley. Over time, these settlements evolved into a centralized state known as Saloum, with its capital at Kahone.

Rise to Power:

Saloum reached its zenith during the 15th and 16th centuries under the leadership of its greatest ruler, Maad Saloum Fode N'Gouye Joof, commonly known as Fode N'Gouye. Fode N'Gouye unified the disparate Serer clans and tribes of Saloum under his rule, establishing a centralized state with a sophisticated administrative system and a strict adherence to Serer religious and cultural traditions. Under his leadership, Saloum became a major center of agriculture, trade, and political power in the Senegambia region.

Economy and Trade:

The economy of Saloum was primarily based on agriculture, with the cultivation of crops such as millet, sorghum, rice, and groundnuts forming the backbone of the economy. The region's fertile soil and abundant water sources supported intensive agriculture, allowing

Saloum to become largely self-sufficient in food production. Trade also played a significant role in the economy, with Saloum serving as a hub for the exchange of goods such as salt, cloth, cattle, and slaves.

Society and Culture:

Saloum society was characterized by its rich cultural heritage, which blended traditional Serer customs and religious beliefs. The Serer people practiced a predominantly agricultural lifestyle, cultivating crops, raising livestock, and fishing in the rivers and lakes of the region. Serer religious and cultural practices were deeply intertwined, with the Serer people maintaining a strong connection to their ancestral spirits, known as "Pangool," and observing traditional rituals and ceremonies to honor them.

• • • •

GOVERNANCE AND ADMINISTRATION:

Saloum was governed by a centralized monarchy, with power vested in the Maad Saloum or king, who was advised by a council of elders and officials. The Maad Saloum's authority was based on a combination of traditional Serer customs and religious beliefs, with justice administered through customary law and arbitration. The kingdom was divided into administrative districts, each governed by appointed officials responsible for taxation, justice, and public works.

Religion and Beliefs:

Serer religious beliefs played a central role in the life and culture of Saloum, with the majority of the population adhering to Serer religion. The Serer people worshipped a pantheon of ancestral spirits, known as "Pangool," who were believed to intercede on behalf of the living and guide their actions. Serer priests, known as "Saltigue," played important roles in religious ceremonies and rituals, serving as mediators between the human and spirit worlds.

Architecture and Urban Planning:

Saloum's architecture was characterized by its traditional Serer-style houses, constructed from locally sourced materials such as mud, thatch, and wood. The kingdom's urban centers were organized around central squares, marketplaces, and shrines, with narrow winding streets connecting different districts. Shrines and sacred sites were focal points of community life, education, and worship, reflecting the region's strong religious and cultural heritage.

Decline and Legacy:

The Kingdom of Saloum began to decline in the 19th century due to internal strife, external pressures, and the encroachment of European colonial powers. The kingdom eventually fell to French colonial forces in the late 19th century, marking the end of its sovereignty as an independent state. However, the legacy of Saloum lives on in the cultural heritage, traditions, and collective memory of the Serer people. The kingdom's contributions to agriculture, trade, and religious beliefs continue to be celebrated and remembered, serving as a source of pride and identity for Serer communities in Senegal and beyond.

The Kingdom of Jolof, also known as the Wolof Empire, was a pre-colonial state located in present-day Senegal, West Africa. Flourishing from the 14th to the 19th century, Jolof played a significant role in the history and culture of the Wolof people, who are primarily known for their agricultural practices, trade networks, and Islamic heritage. In this essay, we will explore the history, economy, society, culture, governance, religion, architecture, and legacy of the Kingdom of Jolof.

Origins and Early History:

The Kingdom of Jolof traces its origins to the medieval period when the Wolof people migrated to the Senegambia region from the south and settled along the banks of the Senegal River. The Wolof established settlements and engaged in agriculture, fishing, and trade, building a network of villages and towns along the river valley. Over time, these settlements coalesced into a centralized state known as Jolof, with its capital at Linguère.

Rise to Power:

Jolof reached its zenith during the 15th and 16th centuries under the leadership of its greatest ruler, Ndiadiane Ndiaye. Ndiadiane Ndiaye unified the disparate Wolof clans and tribes of Jolof under his rule, establishing a centralized state with a sophisticated administrative system and a strict adherence to Islamic law and principles. Under his leadership, Jolof became a major center of trade, agriculture, and political power in the Senegambia region.

Economy and Trade:

The economy of Jolof was primarily based on agriculture, with the cultivation of crops such as millet, sorghum, rice, and groundnuts forming the backbone of the economy. The region's fertile soil and abundant water sources supported intensive agriculture, allowing Jolof to become largely self-sufficient in food production. Trade also played a significant role in the economy, with Jolof serving as a hub for the exchange of goods such as salt, cloth, cattle, and slaves.

Society and Culture:

Jolof society was characterized by its rich cultural heritage, which blended traditional Wolof customs and Islamic beliefs. The Wolof people practiced a predominantly agricultural lifestyle, cultivating crops, raising livestock, and fishing in the rivers and lakes of the region. Islamic education and scholarship were highly valued in Jolof, with Quranic schools, mosques, and Islamic scholars playing important roles in the community. The Wolof language, known as Wolof, was widely spoken, along with Arabic for religious and scholarly purposes.

• • • •

GOVERNANCE AND ADMINISTRATION:

Jolof was governed by a centralized monarchy, with power vested in the Burba Jolof or king, who was advised by a council of elders and officials. The Burba Jolof's authority was based on a combination of traditional Wolof customs and Islamic law, with justice administered through Sharia courts and customary law. The kingdom was divided into administrative districts, each governed by appointed officials responsible for taxation, justice, and public works.

Religion and Beliefs:

Islam played a central role in the life and culture of Jolof, with the majority of the population adhering to Sunni Islam. The Wolof people embraced Islam during the 15th and 16th centuries, following the teachings of Muslim scholars and missionaries who spread the faith across the Senegambia region. Islamic rituals, prayers, and festivals became integral parts of Jolof's cultural identity, shaping its social customs, moral values, and legal practices.

Architecture and Urban Planning:

Jolof's architecture was characterized by its traditional Wolof-style houses, constructed from locally sourced materials such as mud, thatch, and wood. The kingdom's urban centers were organized around central squares, marketplaces, and mosques, with narrow winding streets connecting different districts. Mosques and Quranic schools served as focal points of community life, education, and worship, reflecting the region's strong Islamic heritage.

Decline and Legacy:

The Kingdom of Jolof began to decline in the 19th century due to internal strife, external pressures, and the encroachment of European colonial powers. The kingdom eventually fell to French colonial forces in the late 19th century, marking the end of its sovereignty as an independent state. However, the legacy of Jolof lives on in the cultural heritage, traditions, and collective memory of the Wolof people. The kingdom's contributions to agriculture, trade, and Islamic scholarship continue to be celebrated and remembered, serving as a source of pride and identity for Wolof communities in Senegal and beyond.

Kingdom of Bamum

The Kingdom of Bamum, also known as the Bamum Kingdom or Bamum Sultanate, was a pre-colonial state located in present-day Cameroon, Central Africa. Flourishing from the 17th to the 20th century, Bamum played a significant role in the history and culture of the Bamum people, who are primarily known for their artistic traditions, political organization, and religious practices. In this essay, we will delve into the history, economy, society, culture, governance, religion, architecture, and legacy of the Kingdom of Bamum.

Origins and Early History:

The Kingdom of Bamum traces its origins to the medieval period when the Bamum people migrated to the grasslands of present-day Cameroon and settled in the region around the Tikar Plateau. The Bamum established settlements and engaged in agriculture, cattle herding, and trade, building a network of villages and towns in the area. Over time, these settlements evolved into a centralized state known as Bamum, with its capital at Foumban.

Rise to Power:

Bamum reached its zenith during the 17th and 18th centuries under the leadership of its greatest ruler, Njoya Ibrahim Doh. Njoya Ibrahim Doh unified the disparate Bamum clans and tribes under his rule, establishing a centralized state with a sophisticated administrative system and a strict adherence to traditional Bamum customs and religious beliefs. Under his leadership, Bamum became a major center of trade, art, and political power in the Cameroon Grassfields region.

Economy and Trade:

The economy of Bamum was primarily based on agriculture, with the cultivation of crops such as millet, sorghum, maize, and yams forming the backbone of the economy. The region's fertile soil and favorable climate supported intensive agriculture, allowing Bamum to become largely self-sufficient in food production. Trade also played a significant role in the economy, with Bamum serving as a hub for the exchange of goods such as pottery, textiles, ivory, and gold.

Society and Culture:

Bamum society was characterized by its rich cultural heritage, which blended traditional Bamum customs and religious beliefs. The Bamum people practiced a predominantly agricultural lifestyle, cultivating crops, raising livestock, and engaging in traditional crafts such as pottery, weaving, and metalworking. Art and music were highly valued in Bamum culture, with artists and musicians playing important roles in religious ceremonies, festivals, and rituals.

• • • •

GOVERNANCE AND ADMINISTRATION:

Bamum was governed by a centralized monarchy, with power vested in the Mfon or king, who was advised by a council of elders and officials. The Mfon's authority was based on a combination of traditional Bamum customs and religious beliefs, with justice administered through customary law and arbitration. The kingdom was divided into administrative districts, each governed by appointed officials responsible for taxation, justice, and public works.

Religion and Beliefs:

Traditional Bamum religion played a central role in the life and culture of the kingdom, with the majority of the population adhering to animistic beliefs and practices. The Bamum worshipped a pantheon of ancestral spirits, nature deities, and supernatural beings, who were believed to intercede on behalf of the living and guide their actions. Religious rituals, sacrifices, and ceremonies were important aspects of Bamum society, marking key milestones in the agricultural calendar and life cycle.

Architecture and Urban Planning:

Bamum's architecture was characterized by its traditional mud-brick houses, constructed from locally sourced materials such as clay, straw, and wood. The kingdom's urban centers were organized around central squares, marketplaces, and palaces, with narrow winding streets connecting different districts. Palaces, temples, and ceremonial sites served as focal points of community life, education, and worship, reflecting the region's strong religious and cultural heritage.

Decline and Legacy:

The Kingdom of Bamum began to decline in the late 19th and early 20th centuries due to internal strife, external pressures, and the encroachment of European colonial powers. The kingdom eventually fell to German colonial forces in the early 20th century, marking the end of its sovereignty as an independent state. However, the legacy of Bamum lives on in the cultural heritage, traditions, and collective memory of the Bamum people. The kingdom's contributions to art, culture, and political organization continue to be celebrated and remembered, serving as a source of pride and identity for Bamum communities in Cameroon and beyond.

Kingdom of Bonoman

The Kingdom of Bonoman, also known as Bono Manso, was a significant pre-colonial state situated in what is now present-day Ghana, West Africa. Flourishing from the 11th to the 17th century, Bonoman left an indelible mark on the history, culture, and socio-political landscape of the region. In this essay, we will explore the origins, governance, economy, society, culture, religion, architecture, decline, and lasting legacy of the Kingdom of Bonoman.

Origins and Early History:

The Kingdom of Bonoman was founded by the Akan people, who migrated to the forested regions of present-day Ghana in the medieval period. These early Akan settlers established agricultural communities along the fertile lands of the Brong-Ahafo region. Over time, these settlements evolved into a centralized state with Bono Manso as its capital. The Akan people practiced farming, hunting, and trade, laying the foundations for the emergence of Bonoman as a regional power.

Governance and Administration:

Bonoman was governed by a centralized monarchy led by the Bonohene, or king. The Bonohene wielded considerable authority and was supported by a council of elders and officials. Governance was guided by Akan customary laws and traditions, with justice administered through local courts. The kingdom was organized into administrative districts, each headed by appointed officials responsible for taxation, justice, and public works.

Economy and Trade:

The economy of Bonoman thrived on agriculture, with crops such as yams, plantains, cassava, and cocoa being cultivated. The fertile lands and favorable climate allowed for bountiful harvests, sustaining the kingdom's population. Trade played a significant role in Bonoman's economy, with the kingdom serving as a vital hub for the exchange of goods such as gold, kola nuts, textiles, and slaves. Trade routes connected Bonoman to neighboring regions, facilitating commerce and cultural exchange.

Society and Culture:

Bonoman society was characterized by its rich cultural heritage and social organization. The Akan people practiced a variety of customs, rituals, and ceremonies that underscored their identity and values. Art and craftsmanship flourished in Bonoman, with skilled artisans producing intricate wood carvings, textiles, pottery, and jewelry. Music, dance, and storytelling were integral to Akan culture, serving as means of expression and communication.

Religion and Beliefs:

Religion played a central role in Bonoman society, with the Akan people adhering to traditional beliefs and practices. The Akan worshipped a pantheon of deities known as the Abosom, who were believed to govern various aspects of life. Rituals and sacrifices were performed to honor the Abosom and seek their blessings. Ancestral veneration also held great significance, with reverence paid to deceased ancestors for their guidance and protection.

Architecture and Urban Planning:

Bonoman's architecture was characterized by its traditional Akan-style buildings, constructed from locally sourced materials such as mud, wood, and thatch. Bono Manso, the kingdom's capital, boasted grand palaces, shrines, and administrative structures that reflected the wealth and power of the Bonohene. Urban centers were organized around central squares and marketplaces, with streets connecting different districts. Akan architectural motifs and decorative elements adorned buildings, showcasing the kingdom's artistic prowess.

Decline and Legacy:

The Kingdom of Bonoman began to decline in the 17th century due to internal conflicts, external pressures, and the arrival of European colonial powers. Bonoman eventually became part of the British Gold Coast colony, and later the independent nation of Ghana. Despite its political demise, Bonoman's legacy endures as a testament to the resilience and ingenuity of the Akan people. The kingdom's cultural contributions, including art, religion, and governance, continue to shape Ghanaian identity and heritage to this day. Bonoman remains a source of pride and inspiration for generations of Ghanaians, serving as a reminder of their rich historical legacy.

Kingdom of Dagbon

The Kingdom of Dagbon, located in what is now northern Ghana, stands as a testament to the rich history and cultural heritage of the Dagbamba people. Flourishing from the 11th to the 19th century, Dagbon was a prominent pre-colonial state that played a pivotal role in shaping the socio-political landscape of the region. In this essay, we will delve into the origins, governance, economy, society, culture, religion, architecture, decline, and lasting legacy of the Kingdom of Dagbon.

Origins and Early History:

The Kingdom of Dagbon traces its origins to the 11th century when the Dagbamba people migrated from the Sahel region and settled in the northern savanna plains of present-day Ghana. These early settlers established agricultural communities along the banks of the White Volta River, laying the foundations for the emergence of Dagbon as a distinct political entity. Over time, these settlements coalesced into a centralized state with Yendi as its capital.

Governance and Administration:

Dagbon was governed by a centralized monarchy led by the Ya-Na, or king. The Ya-Na wielded considerable authority and was supported by a council of elders and chiefs. Governance was guided by Dagbon's traditional customs and laws, with justice administered through local courts. The kingdom was divided into administrative districts, each headed by appointed chiefs responsible for maintaining order, collecting taxes, and overseeing public affairs.

Economy and Trade:

The economy of Dagbon was primarily agrarian, with the cultivation of crops such as millet, sorghum, maize, and rice forming the backbone of the economy. The fertile lands and abundant water sources of the White Volta River facilitated agricultural productivity, sustaining the kingdom's population. Trade also played a significant role in Dagbon's economy, with the kingdom serving as a key trading hub for goods such as salt, kola nuts, livestock, and textiles.

Society and Culture:

Dagbon society was characterized by its rich cultural heritage and social organization. The Dagbamba people practiced a variety of customs, rituals, and ceremonies that underscored their identity and values. Extended family networks, known as "sib," formed the basis of social organization, providing support and cohesion within communities. Art and craftsmanship flourished in Dagbon, with skilled artisans producing woven textiles, pottery, and intricate leatherwork.

· · · ·

RELIGION AND BELIEFS:

Religion held a central place in Dagbon society, with the majority of the population adhering to Islam. Islam was introduced to Dagbon through trade and cultural exchange and became deeply ingrained in the kingdom's social fabric. Religious rituals, prayers, and festivals were observed by the Dagbamba people, who also maintained reverence for traditional beliefs and practices. Ancestral veneration and spirit worship were integral aspects of Dagbon's religious landscape, reflecting a syncretic blend of Islamic and indigenous beliefs.

Architecture and Urban Planning:

Dagbon's architecture was characterized by its traditional mud-brick buildings, constructed usinhig locally sourced materials. Yendi, the kingdom's capital, featured grand palaces, mosques, and administrative structures that served as symbols of royal power and prestige. Urban centers were organized around central squares and marketplaces, with winding streets connecting different neighborhoods. Dagbon architecture reflected the kingdom's cultural identity and environmental adaptation.

· · · ·

DECLINE AND LEGACY:

The Kingdom of Dagbon began to decline in the 19th century due to internal conflicts, external pressures, and the incursion of European colonial powers. Dagbon eventually became part of the British Gold Coast colony, and later the independent nation of Ghana. Despite its political demise, Dagbon's legacy endures as a testament to the resilience and cultural heritage of the Dagbamba people. The kingdom's contributions to agriculture, trade, religion, and governance continue to shape Ghanaian society and identity, serving as a source of pride and inspiration for generations to come. Dagbon remains an integral part of Ghana's historical legacy, celebrated for its rich cultural traditions and enduring legacy

Kingdom of Mamprusi

The Kingdom of Mamprusi, situated in present-day northern Ghana, is a significant entity in the annals of West African history. Flourishing from the 17th to the 19th century, Mamprusi stands as a testament to the resilience, cultural richness, and administrative prowess of the Mamprusi people. In this essay, we will explore the origins, governance, economy, society, culture, religion, architecture, decline, and lasting legacy of the Kingdom of Mamprusi.

Origins and Early History:

The Kingdom of Mamprusi traces its origins to the migration of the Mampurugu people from the Mossi Kingdoms in present-day Burkina Faso. These early settlers arrived in the northern savanna plains of what is now Ghana and established agricultural communities along the White Volta River. Over time, these settlements grew into a centralized state with Nalerigu as its capital and the Mamprusi paramountcy at its helm.

Governance and Administration:

Mamprusi was governed by a centralized monarchy led by the Nayiri, or king. The Nayiri wielded considerable authority and was supported by a council of elders and chiefs known as the "Tindana." Governance was guided by Mamprusi's traditional customs and laws, with justice administered through local courts and arbitration. The kingdom was divided into administrative districts, each headed by appointed chiefs responsible for maintaining order, collecting taxes, and overseeing public affairs.

Economy and Trade:

The economy of Mamprusi was predominantly agrarian, with the cultivation of crops such as millet, sorghum, maize, and shea nuts forming the backbone of the economy. The fertile lands and favorable climate of the White Volta River basin supported agricultural productivity, enabling Mamprusi to sustain its population. Trade also played a significant role in Mamprusi's economy, with the kingdom serving as a key trading hub for goods such as salt, kola nuts, cattle, and textiles.

Society and Culture:

Mamprusi society was characterized by its rich cultural heritage and social organization. The Mamprusi people practiced a variety of customs, rituals, and ceremonies that underscored their identity and values. Lineage and kinship ties formed the basis of social organization, with extended family networks providing support and cohesion within communities. Art and craftsmanship flourished in Mamprusi, with skilled artisans producing woven textiles, pottery, and intricate metalwork.

Religion and Beliefs:

Religion held a central place in Mamprusi society, with the majority of the population adhering to Islam. Islam was introduced to Mamprusi through trade and cultural exchange and became deeply entrenched in the kingdom's social fabric. Religious practices, including prayers, fasting, and pilgrimage, were observed by the Mamprusi people, who also maintained reverence for traditional beliefs and practices. Ancestral veneration and spirit worship were integral aspects of Mamprusi's religious landscape, reflecting a syncretic blend of Islamic and indigenous beliefs.

Architecture and Urban Planning:

Mamprusi's architecture was characterized by its traditional mud-brick buildings, constructed using locally sourced materials. Nalerigu, the kingdom's capital, featured grand palaces, mosques, and administrative structures that served as symbols of royal authority and prestige. Urban centers were organized around central squares and marketplaces, with interconnected streets and alleyways. Mamprusi architecture reflected the kingdom's cultural identity and environmental adaptation.

Decline and Legacy:

The Kingdom of Mamprusi began to decline in the 19th century due to internal conflicts, external pressures, and the incursion of European colonial powers. Mamprusi eventually became part of the British Gold Coast colony, and later the independent nation of Ghana. Despite its political demise, Mamprusi's legacy endures as a testament to the resilience and cultural heritage of the Mamprusi people. The kingdom's contributions to agriculture, trade, religion, and governance continue to shape Ghanaian society and identity, serving as a source of pride and inspiration for generations to come. Mamprusi remains an integral part of Ghana's historical legacy, celebrated for its rich cultural traditions and enduring legacy.

The Kingdom of Gonja, located in present-day northern Ghana, is a historical entity with a rich cultural heritage and significant influence in the region. Flourishing from the 16th to the 19th century, Gonja played a pivotal role in shaping the socio-political landscape of northern Ghana. In this essay, we will explore the origins, governance, economy, society, culture, religion, architecture, decline, and lasting legacy of the Kingdom of Gonja.

Origins and Early History:

The Kingdom of Gonja traces its origins to the 16th century when the Mande-speaking people migrated from the Mali Empire and settled in the savanna plains of what is now northern Ghana. These early settlers established agricultural communities along the Black Volta River and its tributaries, laying the foundations for the emergence of Gonja as a distinct political entity. Over time, these settlements grew into a centralized state with Damongo as its capital.

Governance and Administration:

Gonja was governed by a centralized monarchy led by the Yagbonwura, or king. The Yagbonwura wielded considerable authority and was supported by a council of elders and chiefs known as the "Kurumfohene." Governance was guided by Gonja's traditional customs and laws, with justice administered through local courts and arbitration. The kingdom was divided into administrative districts, each headed by appointed chiefs responsible for maintaining order, collecting taxes, and overseeing public affairs.

Economy and Trade:

The economy of Gonja was predominantly agrarian, with the cultivation of crops such as millet, sorghum, maize, and rice forming the backbone of the economy. The fertile lands and favorable climate of the Black Volta River basin supported agricultural productivity, enabling Gonja to sustain its population. Trade also played a significant role in Gonja's economy, with the kingdom serving as a key trading hub for goods such as salt, kola nuts, cattle, and textiles.

Society and Culture:

Gonja society was characterized by its rich cultural heritage and social organization. The Gonja people practiced a variety of customs, rituals, and ceremonies that underscored their identity and values. Lineage and kinship ties formed the basis of social organization, with extended family networks providing support and cohesion within communities. Art and craftsmanship flourished in Gonja, with skilled artisans producing woven textiles, pottery, and intricate leatherwork.

• • • •

RELIGION AND BELIEFS:

Religion held a central place in Gonja society, with the majority of the population adhering to Islam. Islam was introduced to Gonja through trade and cultural exchange and became deeply entrenched in the kingdom's social fabric. Religious practices, including prayers, fasting, and pilgrimage, were observed by the Gonja people, who also maintained reverence for traditional beliefs and practices. Ancestral veneration and spirit worship were integral aspects of Gonja's religious landscape, reflecting a syncretic blend of Islamic and indigenous beliefs.

Architecture and Urban Planning:

Gonja's architecture was characterized by its traditional mud-brick buildings, constructed using locally sourced materials. Damongo, the kingdom's capital, featured grand palaces, mosques, and administrative structures that served as symbols of royal authority and prestige. Urban centers were organized around central squares and marketplaces, with interconnected streets and alleyways. Gonja architecture reflected the kingdom's cultural identity and environmental adaptation.

Decline and Legacy:

The Kingdom of Gonja began to decline in the 19th century due to internal conflicts, external pressures, and the incursion of European colonial powers. Gonja eventually became part of the British Gold Coast colony, and later the independent nation of Ghana. Despite its political demise, Gonja's legacy endures as a testament to the resilience and cultural heritage of the Gonja people. The kingdom's contributions to agriculture, trade, religion, and governance continue to shape Ghanaian society and identity, serving as a source of pride and inspiration for generations to come. Gonja remains an integral part of Ghana's historical legacy, celebrated for its rich cultural traditions and enduring legacy.

Kingdom of Ga

The Kingdom of Ga, situated in present-day Ghana, holds a significant place in the history and cultural heritage of the Ga-Adangbe people. Flourishing from ancient times to the colonial era, the Ga state was renowned for its political organization, cultural vibrancy, and economic significance in the region. In this essay, we will delve into the origins, governance, economy, society, culture, religion, architecture, decline, and lasting legacy of the Kingdom of Ga.

Origins and Early History:

The Kingdom of Ga traces its origins to ancient migrations of the Ga-Adangbe people from the Niger River basin to the coastal plains of present-day Ghana. These early settlers established communities along the Gulf of Guinea, engaging in fishing, farming, and trade. Over time, these settlements coalesced into a centralized state with Accra as its capital, marking the emergence of the Ga Kingdom as a distinct political entity.

Governance and Administration:

Ga was governed by a centralized monarchy led by the Mantse, or king. The Mantse wielded authority and was supported by a council of elders and chiefs known as the "Otublohum." Governance was guided by Ga's traditional customs and laws, with justice administered through local courts and arbitration. The kingdom was divided into administrative districts, each headed by appointed chiefs responsible for maintaining order, collecting taxes, and overseeing public affairs.

Economy and Trade:

The economy of Ga was diverse, with fishing, agriculture, and trade being key sources of livelihood. The coastal location of the kingdom facilitated maritime activities, including fishing and salt production, which contributed to the kingdom's prosperity. Agriculture, particularly the cultivation of cassava, plantains, and maize, also played a significant role in Ga's economy. Trade networks extended inland, connecting Ga with neighboring states and facilitating the exchange of goods such as gold, salt, textiles, and slaves.

Society and Culture:

Ga society was characterized by its rich cultural heritage and social organization. The Ga people practiced a variety of customs, rituals, and ceremonies that underscored their identity and values. Lineage and kinship ties formed the basis of social organization, with extended family networks providing support and cohesion within communities. Art and craftsmanship flourished in Ga, with skilled artisans producing pottery, textiles, and intricate beadwork.

• • • •

RELIGION AND BELIEFS:

Religion held a central place in Ga society, with the majority of the population adhering to indigenous beliefs and practices. The Ga people worshipped a pantheon of deities known as the "Wulomei," who were believed to govern various aspects of life. Religious rituals, ceremonies, and festivals were observed to honor the Wulomei and seek their blessings. Islam and Christianity also gained prominence in Ga society through trade and missionary activities.

Architecture and Urban Planning:

Ga's architecture was characterized by its traditional mud-brick buildings, constructed using locally sourced materials. Accra, the kingdom's capital, featured grand palaces, shrines, and administrative structures that served as symbols of royal authority and prestige. Urban centers were organized around central squares and marketplaces, with interconnected streets and alleys. Ga architecture reflected the kingdom's cultural identity and environmental adaptation.

Decline and Legacy:

The Kingdom of Ga began to decline in the 19th century due to internal conflicts, external pressures, and the incursion of European colonial powers. Ga eventually became part of the British Gold Coast colony, and later the independent nation of Ghana. Despite its political demise, Ga's legacy endures as a testament to the resilience and cultural heritage of the Ga-Adangbe people. The kingdom's contributions to maritime trade, agriculture, religion, and governance continue to shape Ghanaian society and identity, serving as a source of pride and inspiration for generations to come. Ga remains an integral part of Ghana's historical legacy, celebrated for its rich cultural traditions and enduring legacy.

Kingdom of Kuba

The Kingdom of Kuba, also known as the Kingdom of Bushongo, was a powerful and influential state that emerged in Central Africa, present-day Democratic Republic of the Congo (DRC), around the 17th century. Renowned for its rich cultural heritage, complex social organization, and artistic achievements, the Kingdom of Kuba holds a significant place in the history of the region. In this essay, we will explore the origins, governance, economy, society, culture, religion, art, decline, and lasting legacy of the Kingdom of Kuba.

Origins and Early History:

The Kingdom of Kuba traces its origins to the Bantu-speaking peoples who migrated to the region from the north and settled in the fertile lands of the Congo Basin. These early settlers established agricultural communities along the Kasai River and its tributaries, laying the foundations for the emergence of Kuba as a distinct political and cultural entity. Over time, these communities coalesced into a centralized state with the Bushongo people at its core.

Governance and Administration:

Kuba was governed by a centralized monarchy led by the Nyim, or king. The Nyim wielded considerable authority and was supported by a council of nobles and advisors. Governance was guided by Kuba's elaborate system of customary laws and traditions, with justice administered through royal courts and councils. The kingdom was divided into administrative districts, each headed by appointed officials responsible for taxation, justice, and public works.

Economy and Trade:

The economy of Kuba was primarily agrarian, with the cultivation of crops such as millet, sorghum, maize, and cassava forming the backbone of the economy. The fertile soil and abundant rainfall of the Congo Basin supported agricultural productivity, enabling Kuba to sustain its population. Trade also played a significant role in Kuba's economy, with the kingdom serving as a key trading hub for goods such as ivory, copper, cloth, and slaves.

Society and Culture:

Kuba society was characterized by its rich cultural heritage and complex social organization. The Kuba people practiced a variety of customs, rituals, and ceremonies that underscored their identity and values. Lineage and kinship ties formed the basis of social organization, with extended family networks providing support and cohesion within communities. Art and craftsmanship flourished in Kuba, with skilled artisans producing intricate wood carvings, textiles, pottery, and metalwork.

• • • •

RELIGION AND BELIEFS:

Religion held a central place in Kuba society, with the majority of the population adhering to traditional beliefs and practices. The Kuba worshipped a pantheon of deities known as the "Woot," who were believed to govern various aspects of life. Religious rituals, ceremonies, and festivals were observed to honor the Woot and seek their blessings. Ancestral veneration and spirit worship were also integral aspects of Kuba's religious landscape, reflecting a deep connection to the spiritual world.

• • • •

ART AND ARCHITECTURE:

Kuba art and architecture are renowned for their intricacy, symbolism, and aesthetic beauty. Kuba artisans were skilled in a variety of mediums, including wood carving, weaving, pottery, and metalwork. Elaborate masks, sculptures, textiles, and ceremonial objects adorned royal palaces, shrines, and public spaces, serving as expressions of Kuba identity and cultural pride. Kuba art continues to inspire contemporary African artists and scholars alike, reflecting the kingdom's enduring legacy.

Decline and Legacy:

The Kingdom of Kuba began to decline in the late 19th century due to internal conflicts, external pressures, and the impact of European colonialism. Kuba eventually fell under Belgian colonial rule, becoming part of the Congo Free State and later the Belgian Congo. Despite its political demise, Kuba's legacy endures as a testament to the resilience and cultural heritage of the Kuba people. The kingdom's contributions to art, governance, and social organization continue to influence the cultural landscape of Central Africa, serving as a source of pride and inspiration for generations to come. Kuba remains an integral part of the region's historical legacy, celebrated for its rich cultural traditions and enduring legacy.

The Kingdom of Kasanje, situated in present-day Angola, is a historical entity with a rich cultural heritage and significant influence in the region. Flourishing from the 16th to the 19th century, Kasanje played a pivotal role in shaping the socio-political landscape of central Africa. In this essay, we will explore the origins, governance, economy, society, culture, religion, decline, and lasting legacy of the Kingdom of Kasanje.

Origins and Early History:

The Kingdom of Kasanje traces its origins to the Lunda people who migrated from the Kingdom of Lunda in present-day Democratic Republic of the Congo. These early settlers established communities along the Kwango River and its tributaries, engaging in agriculture, trade, and craftsmanship. Over time, these settlements grew into a centralized state with Kasanje as its capital, marking the emergence of the Kasanje Kingdom as a distinct political entity.

Governance and Administration:

Kasanje was governed by a centralized monarchy led by the Mwene, or king. The Mwene wielded considerable authority and was supported by a council of advisors and chiefs. Governance was guided by Kasanje's traditional customs and laws, with justice administered through local courts and councils. The kingdom was divided into administrative districts, each headed by appointed officials responsible for taxation, justice, and public works.

Economy and Trade:

The economy of Kasanje was diverse, with agriculture, trade, and craftsmanship being key sources of wealth. The fertile lands along the Kwango River supported the cultivation of crops such as maize, cassava, peanuts, and palm oil. Trade networks extended across central Africa, connecting Kasanje with neighboring states and facilitating the exchange of goods such as ivory, copper, salt, textiles, and slaves.

Society and Culture:

Kasanje society was characterized by its rich cultural heritage and social organization. The Lunda people practiced a variety of customs, rituals, and ceremonies that underscored their identity and values. Lineage and kinship ties formed the basis of social organization, with extended family networks providing support and cohesion within communities. Art and craftsmanship flourished in Kasanje, with skilled artisans producing woven textiles, pottery, and wood carvings.

Religion and Beliefs:

Religion held a central place in Kasanje society, with the majority of the population adhering to indigenous beliefs and practices. The Lunda people worshipped a pantheon of deities known as the "Kakulu," who were believed to govern various aspects of life. Religious rituals, ceremonies, and festivals were observed to honor the Kakulu and seek their blessings. Ancestral veneration and spirit worship were also integral aspects of Kasanje's religious landscape.

Decline and Legacy:

The Kingdom of Kasanje began to decline in the 19th century due to internal conflicts, external pressures, and the impact of European colonialism. Kasanje eventually fell under Portuguese colonial rule, becoming part of the Portuguese West Africa colony. Despite its political demise, Kasanje's legacy endures as a testament to the resilience and cultural heritage of the Lunda people. The kingdom's contributions to agriculture, trade, religion, and governance continue to shape the cultural landscape of central Africa, serving as a source of pride and inspiration for generations to come. Kasanje remains an integral part of Angola's historical legacy, celebrated for its rich cultural traditions and enduring legacy.

Kingdom of Ndongo

The Kingdom of Ndongo, also known as the Kingdom of Angola, was a powerful and influential state that emerged in present-day Angola during the 16th century. Renowned for its resilience, military prowess, and cultural richness, Ndongo played a significant role in shaping the history of the region. In this essay, we will explore the origins, governance, economy, society, culture, religion, resistance against colonialism, decline, and lasting legacy of the Kingdom of Ndongo.

Origins and Early History:

The Kingdom of Ndongo traces its origins to the Ambundu people who migrated from the Congo Basin to the region of present-day Angola. These early settlers established agricultural communities along the banks of the Kwanza River, engaging in farming, fishing, and trade. Over time, these settlements grew into a centralized state with Kabasa as its capital, marking the emergence of Ndongo as a distinct political entity.

Governance and Administration:

Ndongo was governed by a centralized monarchy led by the Ngola, or king. The Ngola wielded considerable authority and was supported by a council of nobles and advisors. Governance was guided by Ndongo's traditional customs and laws, with justice administered through royal courts and councils. The kingdom was divided into administrative districts, each headed by appointed officials responsible for taxation, justice, and public works.

Economy and Trade:

The economy of Ndongo was predominantly agrarian, with the cultivation of crops such as maize, millet, sorghum, and cassava forming the backbone of the economy. The fertile lands along the Kwanza River supported agricultural productivity, enabling Ndongo to sustain its population. Trade also played a significant role in Ndongo's economy, with the kingdom serving as a key trading hub for goods such as ivory, copper, cloth, and slaves.

Society and Culture:

Ndongo society was characterized by its rich cultural heritage and social organization. The Ambundu people practiced a variety of customs, rituals, and ceremonies that underscored their identity and values. Lineage and kinship ties formed the basis of social organization, with extended family networks providing support and cohesion within communities. Art and craftsmanship flourished in Ndongo, with skilled artisans producing pottery, textiles, and wood carvings.

Religion and Beliefs:

Religion held a central place in Ndongo society, with the majority of the population adhering to indigenous beliefs and practices. The Ambundu people worshipped a pantheon of deities known as the "Sons of Nzambi," who were believed to govern various aspects of life. Religious rituals, ceremonies, and festivals were observed to honor the Sons of Nzambi and seek their blessings. Ancestral veneration and spirit worship were also integral aspects of Ndongo's religious landscape.

Resistance against Colonialism:

Ndongo faced numerous challenges from European colonial powers, particularly the Portuguese, who sought to exploit the kingdom's resources and establish control over the region. Queen Nzinga, one of Ndongo's most notable rulers, led a fierce resistance against Portuguese encroachment, employing military tactics, diplomacy, and alliances with neighboring states. Despite facing setbacks, Queen Nzinga's leadership and resilience inspired generations of Africans and earned her a place in history as a symbol of resistance against colonialism.

Decline and Legacy:

The Kingdom of Ndongo began to decline in the late 17th century due to internal conflicts, external pressures, and the impact of

European colonialism. Ndongo eventually fell under Portuguese control, becoming part of the Portuguese colony of Angola. Despite its political demise, Ndongo's legacy endures as a testament to the resilience and cultural heritage of the Ambundu people. The kingdom's contributions to agriculture, trade, religion, and resistance against colonialism continue to shape the cultural landscape of Angola, serving as a source of pride and inspiration for generations to come. Ndongo remains an integral part of Angola's historical legacy, celebrated for its rich cultural traditions and enduring legacy.

Kingdom of Matamba

The Kingdom of Matamba, located in present-day Angola, was a significant political entity in Central Africa during the 16th to 18th centuries. Renowned for its strategic location, fierce resistance against colonialism, and cultural vibrancy, Matamba played a crucial role in shaping the history of the region. In this essay, we will explore the origins, governance, economy, society, culture, religion, resistance against colonialism, decline, and lasting legacy of the Kingdom of Matamba.

Origins and Early History:

The Kingdom of Matamba traces its origins to the Mbundu people who migrated from the Congo Basin to the region of present-day Angola. These early settlers established agricultural communities along the banks of the Kwanza River and its tributaries, laying the foundations for the emergence of Matamba as a distinct political entity. Over time, these communities coalesced into a centralized state with Matamba as its capital, marking the beginning of the kingdom's history.

Governance and Administration:

Matamba was governed by a centralized monarchy led by the Ngola, or queen. The Ngola wielded considerable authority and was supported by a council of advisors and chiefs. Governance was guided by Matamba's traditional customs and laws, with justice administered through royal courts and councils. The kingdom was divided into administrative districts, each headed by appointed officials responsible for taxation, justice, and public works.

Economy and Trade:

The economy of Matamba was diverse, with agriculture, trade, and craftsmanship being key sources of wealth. The fertile lands along the Kwanza River supported the cultivation of crops such as maize, millet, sorghum, and cassava. Trade networks extended across central Africa, connecting Matamba with neighboring states and facilitating the exchange of goods such as ivory, copper, cloth, and slaves.

Society and Culture:

Matamba society was characterized by its rich cultural heritage and social organization. The Mbundu people practiced a variety of customs, rituals, and ceremonies that underscored their identity and values. Lineage and kinship ties formed the basis of social organization, with extended family networks providing support and cohesion within communities. Art and craftsmanship flourished in Matamba, with skilled artisans producing pottery, textiles, and wood carvings.

Religion and Beliefs:

Religion held a central place in Matamba society, with the majority of the population adhering to indigenous beliefs and practices. The Mbundu people worshipped a pantheon of deities known as the "Mukulu," who were believed to govern various aspects of life. Religious rituals, ceremonies, and festivals were observed to honor the Mukulu and seek their blessings. Ancestral veneration and spirit worship were also integral aspects of Matamba's religious landscape.

Resistance against Colonialism:

Matamba faced numerous challenges from European colonial powers, particularly the Portuguese, who sought to exploit the kingdom's resources and establish control over the region. Queen Njinga, one of Matamba's most notable rulers, led a fierce resistance against Portuguese encroachment, employing military tactics, diplomacy, and alliances with neighboring states. Despite facing setbacks, Queen Njinga's leadership and resilience inspired generations of Africans and earned her a place in history as a symbol of resistance against colonialism.

Decline and Legacy:

The Kingdom of Matamba began to decline in the late 18th century due to internal conflicts, external pressures, and the impact of European colonialism. Matamba eventually fell under Portuguese control, becoming part of the Portuguese colony of Angola. Despite its political demise, Matamba's legacy endures as a testament to the resilience and cultural heritage of the Mbundu people. The kingdom's contributions to agriculture, trade, religion, and resistance against colonialism continue to shape the cultural landscape of Angola, serving as a source of pride and inspiration for generations to come. Matamba remains an integral part of Angola's historical legacy, celebrated for its rich cultural traditions and enduring legacy.

Kingdom of Loango

T he Kingdom of Loango, situated along the Atlantic coast of Central Africa, was a prominent state that emerged during the early modern period. Renowned for its strategic location, maritime trade, and cultural richness, Loango played a significant role in shaping the history and culture of the region. In this essay, we will delve into the origins, governance, economy, society, culture, religion, decline, and lasting legacy of the Kingdom of Loango.

Origins and Early History:

The Kingdom of Loango traces its origins to the Vili people who inhabited the coastal region of present-day Republic of Congo and Angola. These early settlers established fishing villages along the Congo River estuary and engaged in trade with neighboring communities. Over time, these settlements coalesced into a centralized state with Loango as its capital, marking the beginning of the kingdom's history.

Governance and Administration:

Loango was governed by a centralized monarchy led by the Mani, or king. The Mani wielded considerable authority and was supported by a council of nobles and advisors. Governance was guided by Loango's traditional customs and laws, with justice administered through royal courts and councils. The kingdom was divided into administrative districts, each headed by appointed officials responsible for taxation, justice, and public works.

Economy and Trade:

The economy of Loango was primarily based on maritime trade, fishing, and agriculture. The kingdom's strategic location along the Atlantic coast made it a hub for international trade, with merchants from Europe, Africa, and the Americas converging on its shores. Loango exported goods such as ivory, palm oil, textiles, and slaves, while importing luxury items such as firearms, beads, and glassware.

Society and Culture:

Loango society was characterized by its rich cultural heritage and social organization. The Vili people practiced a variety of customs, rituals, and ceremonies that underscored their identity and values. Lineage and kinship ties formed the basis of social organization, with extended family networks providing support and cohesion within communities. Art and craftsmanship flourished in Loango, with skilled artisans producing pottery, textiles, and wood carvings.

Religion and Beliefs:

Religion held a central place in Loango society, with the majority of the population adhering to indigenous beliefs and practices. The Vili people worshipped a pantheon of deities known as the "Bembe," who were believed to govern various aspects of life. Religious rituals, ceremonies, and festivals were observed to honor the Bembe and seek their blessings. Ancestral veneration and spirit worship were also integral aspects of Loango's religious landscape.

Decline and Legacy:

The Kingdom of Loango began to decline in the 19th century due to internal conflicts, external pressures, and the impact of European colonialism. Loango eventually fell under French colonial rule, becoming part of French Equatorial Africa. Despite its political demise, Loango's legacy endures as a testament to the resilience and cultural heritage of the Vili people. The kingdom's contributions to maritime trade, art, religion, and governance continue to shape the cultural landscape of Central Africa, serving as a source of pride and inspiration for generations to come. Loango remains an integral part of the region's historical legacy, celebrated for its rich cultural traditions and enduring legacy.

Kingdom of Kilwa

The Kingdom of Kilwa, situated along the Swahili Coast of East Africa, was a powerful and influential state that emerged in the 10th century. Renowned for its strategic location, maritime trade, and cultural richness, Kilwa played a significant role in shaping the history and economy of the Indian Ocean region. In this essay, we will explore the origins, governance, economy, society, culture, religion, decline, and lasting legacy of the Kingdom of Kilwa.

Origins and Early History:

The Kingdom of Kilwa traces its origins to the Swahili people who inhabited the coastal region of present-day Tanzania. These early settlers established fishing villages and engaged in maritime trade with other civilizations along the Indian Ocean coast. Over time, these settlements grew into a centralized state with Kilwa as its capital, marking the beginning of the kingdom's history.

Governance and Administration:

Kilwa was governed by a centralized monarchy led by the Sultan, who wielded considerable authority and was supported by a council of advisors and officials. Governance was guided by Kilwa's traditional customs and laws, with justice administered through royal courts and councils. The kingdom was divided into administrative districts, each headed by appointed officials responsible for taxation, justice, and public works.

Economy and Trade:

The economy of Kilwa was primarily based on maritime trade, fishing, and agriculture. The kingdom's strategic location along the Swahili Coast made it a hub for international trade, with merchants from Asia, Africa, and the Middle East converging on its shores. Kilwa exported goods such as gold, ivory, copper, iron, and slaves, while importing luxury items such as porcelain, silk, spices, and textiles.

Society and Culture:

Kilwa society was characterized by its rich cultural heritage and social organization. The Swahili people practiced a variety of customs, rituals, and ceremonies that underscored their identity and values. Lineage and kinship ties formed the basis of social organization, with extended family networks providing support and cohesion within communities. Art and craftsmanship flourished in Kilwa, with skilled artisans producing pottery, textiles, and wood carvings.

Religion and Beliefs:

Religion held a central place in Kilwa society, with the majority of the population adhering to Islam. The Swahili people embraced the teachings of Islam, which spread to the region through trade and contact with Muslim merchants and scholars. Mosques and madrasas were established in Kilwa, where Islamic law and theology were taught. Religious festivals and ceremonies were observed to honor Islamic traditions and values.

Decline and Legacy:

The Kingdom of Kilwa began to decline in the 16th century due to internal conflicts, external pressures, and the impact of Portuguese colonialism. Kilwa eventually fell under Portuguese control, becoming part of the Portuguese East Africa colony. Despite its political demise, Kilwa's legacy endures as a testament to the resilience and cultural heritage of the Swahili people. The kingdom's contributions to maritime trade, architecture, religion, and governance continue to shape the cultural landscape of East Africa, serving as a source of pride and inspiration for generations to come. Kilwa remains an integral part of Tanzania's historical legacy, celebrated for its rich cultural traditions and enduring legacy along the Swahili Coast.

Kingdom of Maravi

The Kingdom of Maravi, also known as the Maravi Empire, was a significant political entity that emerged in present-day Malawi and parts of Zambia and Mozambique during the 15th century. Renowned for its military strength, economic prosperity, and cultural achievements, Maravi played a crucial role in shaping the history and identity of the region. In this essay, we will explore the origins, governance, economy, society, culture, religion, decline, and lasting legacy of the Kingdom of Maravi.

• • • •

ORIGINS AND EARLY HISTORY:

The Kingdom of Maravi traces its origins to the Bantu-speaking peoples who migrated to the region from the north and settled in the fertile lands of the Shire Highlands and Lake Malawi. These early settlers established agricultural communities and engaged in trade with neighboring states. Over time, these communities coalesced into a centralized state with Maravi as its capital, marking the beginning of the kingdom's history.

Governance and Administration:

Maravi was governed by a centralized monarchy led by the Mwene, or king. The Mwene wielded considerable authority and was supported by a council of advisors and officials. Governance was guided by Maravi's traditional customs and laws, with justice administered through royal courts and councils. The kingdom was divided into administrative districts, each headed by appointed officials responsible for taxation, justice, and public works.

Economy and Trade:

The economy of Maravi was primarily agrarian, with the cultivation of crops such as millet, sorghum, maize, and tobacco forming the backbone of the economy. The fertile soils of the Shire Highlands and the shores of Lake Malawi supported agricultural productivity, enabling Maravi to sustain its population. Trade also played a significant role in Maravi's economy, with the kingdom serving as a key trading hub for goods such as ivory, copper, salt, and slaves.

Society and Culture:

Maravi society was characterized by its rich cultural heritage and social organization. The Chewa people, who were the dominant ethnic group in Maravi, practiced a variety of customs, rituals, and ceremonies that underscored their identity and values. Lineage and kinship ties formed the basis of social organization, with extended family networks providing support and cohesion within communities. Art and craftsmanship flourished in Maravi, with skilled artisans producing pottery, textiles, and wood carvings.

Religion and Beliefs:

Religion held a central place in Maravi society, with the majority of the population adhering to indigenous beliefs and practices. The Chewa people worshipped a pantheon of ancestral spirits and nature deities, who were believed to govern various aspects of life. Religious rituals, ceremonies, and festivals were observed to honor the spirits and seek their blessings. Ancestral veneration and spirit worship were also integral aspects of Maravi's religious landscape.

Decline and Legacy:

The Kingdom of Maravi began to decline in the 18th century due to internal conflicts, external pressures, and the impact of European colonialism. Maravi eventually fell under British colonial rule, becoming part of the British Central Africa Protectorate, which later became Nyasaland and eventually Malawi. Despite its political demise, Maravi's legacy endures as a testament to the resilience and cultural heritage of the Chewa people. The kingdom's contributions to agriculture, trade, religion, and governance continue to shape the cultural landscape of Malawi and the wider region, serving as a source of pride and inspiration for generations to come. Maravi remains an integral part of Malawi's historical legacy, celebrated for its rich cultural traditions and enduring legacy in the heart of Africa.

Kingdom of Nri

The Kingdom of Nri, located in present-day southeastern Nigeria, was a pre-colonial state that emerged around the 10th century. Renowned for its unique political system, spiritual significance, and cultural influence, Nri played a significant role in shaping the history and identity of the Igbo people. In this essay, we will explore the origins, governance, economy, society, culture, religion, decline, and lasting legacy of the Kingdom of Nri.

Origins and Early History:

The Kingdom of Nri traces its origins to the ancient Igbo people who inhabited the forests and savannas of southeastern Nigeria. According to oral tradition, Nri was founded by Eri, a mythical figure believed to be the ancestor of the Igbo people. The kingdom emerged as a result of the consolidation of smaller chiefdoms under the authority of the Eze Nri, or king of Nri.

Governance and Administration:

Nri was governed by a unique political system characterized by a theocratic monarchy. The Eze Nri, who held both political and spiritual authority, was regarded as a divine ruler with a sacred mandate to govern. Governance was guided by Nri's traditional customs and laws, which were enforced through a council of titled officials and village chiefs. The kingdom was divided into administrative districts, each headed by appointed officials responsible for taxation, justice, and public works.

Economy and Trade:

The economy of Nri was predominantly agrarian, with the cultivation of crops such as yams, cassava, and palm oil forming the backbone of the economy. The fertile lands of southeastern Nigeria supported agricultural productivity, enabling Nri to sustain its population. Trade also played a significant role in Nri's economy, with the kingdom serving as a key trading hub for goods such as salt, ivory, copper, and slaves.

Society and Culture:

Nri society was characterized by its rich cultural heritage and social organization. The Igbo people practiced a variety of customs, rituals, and ceremonies that underscored their identity and values. Lineage and kinship ties formed the basis of social organization, with extended family networks providing support and cohesion within communities. Art and craftsmanship flourished in Nri, with skilled artisans producing pottery, textiles, and wood carvings.

Religion and Beliefs:

Religion held a central place in Nri society, with the Eze Nri serving as both a political and spiritual leader. The Igbo people worshipped a pantheon of deities known as the Alusi, who were believed to govern various aspects of life. Religious rituals, ceremonies, and festivals were observed to honor the Alusi and seek their blessings. Ancestral veneration and spirit worship were also integral aspects of Nri's religious landscape.

Decline and Legacy:

The Kingdom of Nri began to decline in the 19th century due to internal conflicts, external pressures, and the impact of British colonialism. Nri eventually fell under British rule, becoming part of the British colony of Nigeria. Despite its political demise, Nri's legacy endures as a testament to the resilience and cultural heritage of the Igbo people. The kingdom's unique political system, spiritual significance, and cultural influence continue to shape the identity and traditions of southeastern Nigeria, serving as a source of pride and inspiration for generations to come. Nri remains an integral part of Nigeria's historical legacy, celebrated for its rich cultural traditions and enduring legacy in the heart of Igbo land.

Kingdom of Imerina

The Kingdom of Imerina, located on the island of Madagascar, was a powerful and influential state that emerged in the central highlands during the 16th century. Renowned for its strategic location, innovative governance, and cultural richness, Imerina played a significant role in shaping the history and identity of the Malagasy people. In this essay, we will explore the origins, governance, economy, society, culture, religion, decline, and lasting legacy of the Kingdom of Imerina.

Origins and Early History:

The Kingdom of Imerina traces its origins to the Merina people, who migrated to the central highlands of Madagascar from the coast in the 15th century. These early settlers established agricultural communities and engaged in trade with neighboring regions. Over time, these settlements grew into a centralized state with Imerina as its heartland, marking the beginning of the kingdom's history.

Governance and Administration:

Imerina was governed by a centralized monarchy led by the Andriana, or noble class. The Andriana wielded considerable authority and were supported by a council of advisors and officials. Governance was guided by Imerina's traditional customs and laws, with justice administered through royal courts and councils. The kingdom was divided into administrative districts, each headed by appointed officials responsible for taxation, justice, and public works.

Economy and Trade:

The economy of Imerina was primarily agrarian, with the cultivation of rice, maize, and other crops forming the backbone of the economy. The fertile lands of the central highlands supported agricultural productivity, enabling Imerina to sustain its population. Trade also played a significant role in Imerina's economy, with the kingdom serving as a key trading hub for goods such as cattle, honey, textiles, and slaves.

Society and Culture:

Imerina society was characterized by its rich cultural heritage and social organization. The Merina people practiced a variety of customs, rituals, and ceremonies that underscored their identity and values. Lineage and kinship ties formed the basis of social organization, with extended family networks providing support and cohesion within communities. Art and craftsmanship flourished in Imerina, with skilled artisans producing pottery, textiles, and wood carvings.

Religion and Beliefs:

Religion held a central place in Imerina society, with the majority of the population adhering to indigenous beliefs and practices. The Merina people worshipped a pantheon of ancestral spirits and nature deities, who were believed to govern various aspects of life. Religious rituals, ceremonies, and festivals were observed to honor the spirits and seek their blessings. Ancestral veneration and spirit worship were also integral aspects of Imerina's religious landscape.

Decline and Legacy:

The Kingdom of Imerina began to decline in the 19th century due to internal conflicts, external pressures, and the impact of European colonialism. Imerina eventually fell under French colonial rule, becoming part of the colony of Madagascar. Despite its political demise, Imerina's legacy endures as a testament to the resilience and cultural heritage of the Merina people. The kingdom's contributions to agriculture, trade, religion, and governance continue to shape the cultural landscape of Madagascar, serving as a source of pride and inspiration for generations to come. Imerina remains an integral part of Madagascar's historical legacy, celebrated for its rich cultural traditions and enduring legacy in the central highlands.

Kingdom of Sakalava

The Kingdom of Sakalava, situated in western Madagascar, was a significant political entity that emerged during the 16th century. Renowned for its maritime prowess, military strength, and cultural richness, the Sakalava kingdom played a pivotal role in shaping the history and identity of the Malagasy people. In this essay, we will explore the origins, governance, economy, society, culture, religion, decline, and lasting legacy of the Kingdom of Sakalava.

Origins and Early History:

The Kingdom of Sakalava traces its origins to the Sakalava people, an ethnic group inhabiting the western coast of Madagascar. The Sakalava emerged as a distinct cultural and political entity through the consolidation of various chiefdoms and clans in the region. By the 16th century, the Sakalava kingdom had established itself as a formidable power along the coast, with control over trade routes and maritime activities.

Governance and Administration:

Sakalava was governed by a decentralized system of rule, with power vested in local chiefs known as "mpivarotra" or "mpanjaka." These chiefs exercised authority over their respective territories, overseeing matters of justice, administration, and defense. While the Sakalava kingdom lacked a centralized monarchy, alliances and confederations were formed among different Sakalava chieftains to coordinate military campaigns and address common challenges.

Economy and Trade:

The economy of the Sakalava kingdom was heavily reliant on maritime trade, fishing, and agriculture. The Sakalava people were skilled sailors and navigators, adept at exploiting the rich resources of the Indian Ocean. They engaged in trade with neighboring islands and the mainland, exchanging commodities such as cattle, rice, salt, spices, and slaves. Sakalava ports served as vital hubs for commerce, attracting merchants from across the region.

Society and Culture:

Sakalava society was characterized by its rich cultural heritage and social organization. The Sakalava people practiced a variety of customs, rituals, and ceremonies that underscored their identity and values. Lineage and kinship ties played a significant role in social organization, with clan affiliations determining one's status and obligations within the community. Art and craftsmanship flourished among the Sakalava, with skilled artisans producing intricate woodcarvings, textiles, and pottery.

Religion and Beliefs:

Religion held a central place in Sakalava society, with a complex belief system influenced by indigenous animism, ancestor worship, and Islamic traditions. The Sakalava worshipped a pantheon of ancestral spirits, nature deities, and Muslim saints, whom they believed exerted influence over their lives. Religious rituals, ceremonies, and festivals were observed to honor the spirits and seek their protection and guidance in various endeavors.

Decline and Legacy:

The Kingdom of Sakalava experienced a gradual decline in the 19th century due to internal conflicts, external pressures, and the impact of European colonialism. The arrival of European powers, particularly the French, disrupted traditional trade networks and undermined Sakalava autonomy. Eventually, Sakalava territories were incorporated into the French colony of Madagascar. Despite its political demise, the legacy of the Sakalava kingdom endures as a testament to the resilience, ingenuity, and maritime prowess of the Malagasy people. The kingdom's contributions to trade, culture, and society continue to shape the identity and heritage of western Madagascar, serving as a source of pride and inspiration for generations to come. Sakalava remains an integral part of Madagascar's historical legacy, celebrated for its rich cultural traditions and enduring legacy along the western coast.

Azanda Kingdom

The Azande Kingdom, situated in present-day South Sudan, the Democratic Republic of the Congo, and the Central African Republic, was a powerful and influential state that emerged in the 18th century. Renowned for its military prowess, political organization, and rich cultural heritage, the Azande Kingdom played a significant role in shaping the history and identity of the Central African region. In this essay, we will explore the origins, governance, economy, society, culture, religion, decline, and lasting legacy of the Azande Kingdom.

Origins and Early History:

The Azande Kingdom traces its origins to the Azande people, an ethnic group that migrated from the Nile Valley region into central Africa around the 16th century. The Azande settled in the fertile lands along the borders of present-day South Sudan, the Democratic Republic of the Congo, and the Central African Republic. Over time, they established a series of chiefdoms and small kingdoms, which eventually coalesced into the Azande Kingdom under the leadership of Gbudwe, a legendary ruler who united the Azande tribes.

Governance and Administration:

The Azande Kingdom was governed by a centralized monarchy led by the Nzara, or king, who wielded supreme authority over the kingdom. The Nzara was supported by a council of advisors, nobles, and warriors who assisted in the administration of state affairs. Governance was guided by Azande's traditional customs and laws, with justice administered through local courts and councils. The kingdom was divided into administrative districts, each overseen by appointed officials responsible for taxation, justice, and public works.

Economy and Trade:

The economy of the Azande Kingdom was predominantly agrarian, with the cultivation of crops such as sorghum, millet, and cassava forming the backbone of the economy. The fertile soils of the region supported agricultural productivity, enabling the Azande to sustain their population and support urban centers. Trade also played a significant role in the Azande economy, with the kingdom serving as a key trading hub for goods such as ivory, slaves, gold, and salt.

Society and Culture:

Azande society was characterized by its rich cultural heritage and social organization. The Azande people practiced a variety of customs, rituals, and ceremonies that underscored their identity and values. Lineage and kinship ties played a significant role in social organization, with extended family networks providing support and cohesion within communities. Art and craftsmanship flourished among the Azande, with skilled artisans producing intricate wood carvings, pottery, and textiles.

Religion and Beliefs:

Religion held a central place in Azande society, with the majority of the population adhering to indigenous animist beliefs. The Azande worshipped a pantheon of ancestral spirits, nature deities, and forest spirits, whom they believed exerted influence over their lives. Religious rituals, ceremonies, and sacrifices were conducted to honor the spirits and seek their protection and guidance in various endeavors. Ancestral veneration and spirit worship were also integral aspects of Azande's religious landscape.

Decline and Legacy:

The Azande Kingdom began to decline in the late 19th century due to internal conflicts, external pressures, and the impact of European colonialism. The kingdom eventually fell under colonial rule, becoming part of various European colonies in central Africa. Despite its political demise, the legacy of the Azande Kingdom endures as a testament to the resilience and cultural heritage of the Azande people. The kingdom's contributions to agriculture, trade, religion, and governance continue to shape the cultural landscape of central Africa, serving as a source of pride and inspiration for generations to come. The

Azande remain an integral part of the cultural tapestry of the region, celebrated for their rich traditions, vibrant culture, and enduring legacy as one of the great civilizations of central Africa.

The Shilluk Kingdom, situated in present-day South Sudan along the banks of the White Nile, was a significant political and cultural entity that emerged in the 15th century. Renowned for its complex social organization, military prowess, and rich cultural heritage, the Shilluk Kingdom played a central role in shaping the history and identity of the region. In this essay, we will explore the origins, governance, economy, society, culture, religion, decline, and lasting legacy of the Shilluk Kingdom.

Origins and Early History:

The Shilluk Kingdom traces its origins to the Shilluk people, a Nilotic ethnic group that migrated from the north into the Upper Nile region around the 15th century. The Shilluk settled along the banks of the White Nile, where they established a series of chiefdoms and small kingdoms. Over time, these chiefdoms coalesced into a unified kingdom under the leadership of Nyikang, a legendary figure who is revered as the founder of the Shilluk Kingdom.

Governance and Administration:

The Shilluk Kingdom was governed by a centralized monarchy led by the Reth, or king, who wielded supreme authority over the kingdom. The Reth was supported by a council of chiefs, advisors, and elders who assisted in the administration of state affairs. Governance was guided by Shilluk's traditional customs and laws, with justice administered through local courts and councils. The kingdom was divided into administrative districts, each overseen by appointed officials responsible for taxation, justice, and public works.

Economy and Trade:

The economy of the Shilluk Kingdom was predominantly agrarian, with the cultivation of sorghum, millet, and maize forming the backbone of the economy. The fertile soils of the Nile floodplain supported agricultural productivity, enabling the Shilluk to sustain their population and support urban centers. Trade also played a significant role in the Shilluk economy, with the kingdom serving as a key trading hub for goods such as cattle, ivory, slaves, and agricultural produce.

Society and Culture:

Shilluk society was characterized by its complex social organization and rich cultural traditions. The Shilluk people practiced a variety of customs, rituals, and ceremonies that underscored their identity and values. Lineage and kinship ties played a significant role in social organization, with extended family networks providing support and cohesion within communities. Art and craftsmanship flourished among the Shilluk, with skilled artisans producing intricate pottery, weaving, and metalwork.

· · · ·

RELIGION AND BELIEFS:

Religion held a central place in Shilluk society, with the majority of the population adhering to indigenous animist beliefs. The Shilluk worshipped a pantheon of ancestral spirits, nature deities, and guardian spirits, whom they believed exerted influence over their lives. Religious rituals, ceremonies, and sacrifices were conducted to honor the spirits and seek their protection and guidance in various endeavors. Ancestral veneration and spirit worship were also integral aspects of Shilluk's religious landscape.

Decline and Legacy:

The Shilluk Kingdom began to decline in the late 19th century due to internal conflicts, external pressures, and the impact of European colonialism. The kingdom eventually fell under colonial rule, becoming part of the Anglo-Egyptian Sudan. Despite its political demise, the legacy of the Shilluk Kingdom endures as a testament to the resilience and cultural heritage of the Shilluk people. The kingdom's contributions to agriculture, trade, religion, and governance continue to shape the cultural landscape of South Sudan, serving as a source of pride and inspiration for generations to come. The Shilluk remain an integral part of the cultural tapestry of the region, celebrated for their rich traditions, vibrant culture, and enduring legacy as one of the great civilizations of East Africa.

The Anyuak Kingdom, located in present-day South Sudan and Ethiopia along the banks of the Baro River, was a notable political and cultural entity that emerged in the 17th century. Renowned for its distinctive social structure, agricultural expertise, and rich cultural heritage, the Anyuak Kingdom played a significant role in shaping the history and identity of the region. In this essay, we will explore the origins, governance, economy, society, culture, religion, decline, and lasting legacy of the Anyuak Kingdom.

Origins and Early History:

The Anyuak Kingdom traces its origins to the Anyuak people, an ethnic group belonging to the Nilotic Luo family. The Anyuak are believed to have migrated from the Upper Nile region into the fertile lands along the Baro River during the 17th century. They settled in small villages and established a decentralized system of governance based on kinship ties and clan affiliation.

Governance and Administration:

The Anyuak Kingdom was characterized by a decentralized system of rule, with power distributed among various clan leaders and elders. Each clan, known as a "jok," was led by a chief or "joka" who exercised authority over his extended family and territory. Governance was guided by traditional customs and laws, with disputes resolved through consensus-based decision-making and mediation by clan leaders. While there was no centralized monarchy, alliances and alliances were formed among different clans to address common challenges and conflicts.

Economy and Trade:

The economy of the Anyuak Kingdom was primarily agrarian, with the Anyuak people practicing subsistence agriculture supplemented by fishing, hunting, and gathering. The fertile lands along the Baro River supported the cultivation of crops such as sorghum, maize, millet, and cassava, which formed the staple diet of the population. Trade with neighboring communities, including the Nuer and Anuak, facilitated the exchange of goods such as livestock, grains, pottery, and handicrafts.

Society and Culture:

Anyuak society was characterized by its rich cultural traditions, social cohesion, and egalitarian ethos. Lineage and kinship ties played a central role in social organization, with extended family networks providing support and solidarity within communities. Anyuak villages were organized around communal structures, including meeting halls and ritual spaces, where important social and religious ceremonies took place. Art and craftsmanship flourished among the Anyuak, with skilled artisans producing intricate pottery, woven textiles, and wood carvings.

Religion and Beliefs:

Religion held a central place in Anyuak society, with the majority of the population adhering to indigenous animist beliefs. The Anyuak worshipped a pantheon of ancestral spirits, nature deities, and guardian spirits, whom they believed exerted influence over their lives. Religious rituals, ceremonies, and sacrifices were conducted to honor the spirits and seek their protection and guidance in various endeavors. Ancestral veneration and spirit worship were integral aspects of Anyuak's religious landscape, with ceremonies performed to appease the spirits and ensure the well-being of the community.

Decline and Legacy:

The Anyuak Kingdom experienced significant upheaval and transformation in the late 19th and early 20th centuries due to the impact of colonialism, migration, and internal conflicts. The region was eventually incorporated into the territories of modern-day South Sudan and Ethiopia, leading to changes in governance, land tenure, and cultural practices. Despite these challenges, the legacy of the Anyuak Kingdom endures as a testament to the resilience, cultural heritage, and enduring spirit of the Anyuak people. The kingdom's contributions to agriculture, trade, religion, and social organization continue to shape the cultural landscape of South Sudan and Ethiopia, serving as a source of pride and inspiration for generations to come. The Anyuak remain an integral part of the cultural tapestry of the region, celebrated for their rich traditions, vibrant culture, and enduring legacy as one of the great civilizations of East Africa.

Fur Sultanate

The Fur Sultanate, located in present-day Darfur region of western Sudan, was a significant political and cultural entity that emerged in the 17th century. Renowned for its military prowess, administrative organization, and rich cultural heritage, the Fur Sultanate played a central role in shaping the history and identity of the region. In this essay, we will explore the origins, governance, economy, society, culture, religion, decline, and lasting legacy of the Fur Sultanate.

Origins and Early History:

The Fur Sultanate traces its origins to the Fur people, an ethnic group indigenous to the Darfur region of western Sudan. The Fur are believed to have migrated to the area in ancient times, settling in the fertile lands along the southern slopes of the Jebel Marra mountains. Over time, the Fur established a series of chiefdoms and small kingdoms, which eventually coalesced into the Fur Sultanate under the leadership of the Tunjur dynasty.

Governance and Administration:

The Fur Sultanate was governed by a centralized monarchy led by the Sultan, who wielded supreme authority over the kingdom. The Sultan was supported by a council of advisors, nobles, and administrators who assisted in the governance of state affairs. Governance was guided by Fur's traditional customs and laws, with justice administered through local courts and councils. The kingdom was divided into administrative districts, each overseen by appointed officials responsible for taxation, justice, and public works.

Economy and Trade:

The economy of the Fur Sultanate was predominantly agrarian, with the cultivation of millet, sorghum, and other crops forming the backbone of the economy. The fertile soils of the Jebel Marra mountains supported agricultural productivity, enabling the Fur to sustain their population and support urban centers. Trade also played a significant role in the Fur economy, with the kingdom serving as a key trading hub for goods such as ivory, slaves, gold, and salt.

Society and Culture:

Fur society was characterized by its rich cultural heritage and social organization. The Fur people practiced a variety of customs, rituals, and ceremonies that underscored their identity and values. Lineage and kinship ties played a significant role in social organization, with extended family networks providing support and cohesion within communities. Art and craftsmanship flourished among the Fur, with skilled artisans producing intricate pottery, weaving, and metalwork.

• • • •

RELIGION AND BELIEFS:

Religion held a central place in Fur society, with the majority of the population adhering to indigenous animist beliefs. The Fur worshipped a pantheon of ancestral spirits, nature deities, and guardian spirits, whom they believed exerted influence over their lives. Religious rituals, ceremonies, and sacrifices were conducted to honor the spirits and seek their protection and guidance in various endeavors. Ancestral veneration and spirit worship were integral aspects of Fur's religious landscape.

Decline and Legacy:

The Fur Sultanate began to decline in the late 19th century due to internal conflicts, external pressures, and the impact of European colonialism. The kingdom eventually fell under colonial rule, becoming part of the Anglo-Egyptian Sudan. Despite its political demise, the legacy of the Fur Sultanate endures as a testament to the resilience and cultural heritage of the Fur people. The kingdom's contributions to agriculture, trade, religion, and governance continue to shape the cultural landscape of Sudan, serving as a source of pride and inspiration for generations to come. The Fur remain an integral part of the cultural tapestry of the region, celebrated for their rich traditions, vibrant culture, and enduring legacy as one of the great civilizations of Africa.

The Zulu Empire, situated in present-day South Africa, is one of Africa's most renowned and influential civilizations. Emerging in the early 19th century under the leadership of the legendary King Shaka Zulu, the Zulu Empire left an indelible mark on the history and culture of southern Africa. In this essay, we will explore the origins, governance, military prowess, society, culture, religion, decline, and lasting legacy of the Zulu Empire.

Origins and Early History:

The origins of the Zulu people can be traced back to the Bantu migrations that swept across southern Africa over millennia. The Zulu tribe emerged as one of the prominent clans of the Nguni people, who settled in the region that would later become known as KwaZulu-Natal. By the late 18th century, the Zulu tribe had established itself as a formidable force in the region under the leadership of Chief Senzangakhona.

Rise of the Zulu Empire:

The transformation of the Zulu tribe into a formidable empire began with the ascent of King Shaka Zulu in the early 19th century. Shaka, a brilliant military strategist and visionary leader, revolutionized Zulu warfare by introducing innovative tactics, weaponry, and organizational reforms. Under his leadership, the Zulu army, known as the Impi, became a formidable fighting force that conquered and assimilated neighboring tribes, expanding the boundaries of the Zulu Empire.

Governance and Administration:

The Zulu Empire was governed by a centralized monarchy headed by the king, who wielded absolute authority over the kingdom. The king was supported by a council of advisors, military commanders, and clan elders who assisted in the administration of state affairs. Governance was guided by traditional customs and laws, with justice administered through tribal courts and councils. The kingdom was divided into administrative districts, each overseen by appointed officials responsible for taxation, justice, and defense.

Military Prowess:

The military prowess of the Zulu Empire was legendary, thanks largely to the innovative tactics and strategies devised by King Shaka. Shaka revolutionized Zulu warfare by introducing the "buffalo horn" formation, a highly effective tactic that involved encircling and overwhelming enemy forces. The Zulu army, armed with the iconic short stabbing spear known as the assegai, was renowned for its discipline, agility, and ferocity in battle. Through a series of military campaigns and conquests, the Zulu Empire established itself as the dominant power in southern Africa.

Society and Culture:

Zulu society was organized along hierarchical lines, with the king at the apex of the social pyramid, followed by the nobility, warriors, commoners, and slaves. Kinship ties and clan affiliations played a significant role in social organization, providing cohesion and stability within communities. Zulu culture was characterized by rich traditions, including music, dance, storytelling, and oral poetry. The Zulu people were skilled artisans, known for their intricate beadwork, pottery, and weaving.

Religion and Beliefs:

Religion held a central place in Zulu society, with the majority of the population adhering to indigenous animist beliefs. The Zulu worshipped a pantheon of ancestral spirits, nature deities, and guardian spirits, whom they believed exerted influence over their lives. Religious rituals, ceremonies, and sacrifices were conducted to honor the spirits and seek their protection and guidance in various endeavors. Ancestral veneration and spirit worship were integral aspects of Zulu's religious landscape.

Decline and Legacy:

The Zulu Empire began to decline in the late 19th century due to internal conflicts, external pressures, and the impact of European colonialism. The kingdom eventually fell under British rule, becoming part of the Union of South Africa in 1910. Despite its political demise, the legacy of the Zulu Empire endures as a testament to the resilience, military prowess, and cultural heritage of the Zulu people. The kingdom's contributions to warfare, governance, and cultural expression continue to shape the identity and pride of the Zulu nation, serving as a source of inspiration for generations to come.

Egyptian Empire

The Egyptian Empire, also known as Ancient Egypt, is one of the most iconic and influential civilizations in human history. Stretching back over five millennia, Egypt's rich cultural heritage, monumental architecture, and advanced civilization have left an indelible mark on the world. In this essay, we will explore the origins, governance, economy, society, culture, religion, decline, and lasting legacy of the Egyptian Empire.

Origins and Early History:

Ancient Egypt traces its origins to the banks of the Nile River, where the civilization emerged around 3100 BCE during the Early Dynastic Period. The unification of Upper and Lower Egypt under King Menes marked the beginning of the First Dynasty and the establishment of the Egyptian state. Over the centuries, Egypt flourished as a powerful empire, ruled by a succession of pharaohs, and became one of the cradles of human civilization.

Governance and Administration:

The Egyptian Empire was governed by a centralized monarchy headed by the pharaoh, who was believed to be the divine ruler chosen by the gods to lead the people. The pharaoh wielded absolute authority over the kingdom and was revered as both a political and religious figure. Governance was administered through a complex bureaucracy composed of viziers, scribes, and officials who managed the affairs of state, collected taxes, and oversaw public works projects such as irrigation systems, temples, and monuments.

Economy and Trade:

The economy of Ancient Egypt was primarily agrarian, with the fertile lands of the Nile Delta and Valley supporting abundant agricultural production. The cultivation of crops such as wheat, barley, flax, and papyrus formed the foundation of Egypt's economy, providing sustenance for the population and surplus for trade. Egypt's strategic location at the crossroads of Africa, Asia, and Europe facilitated extensive trade networks, enabling the exchange of goods such as gold, incense, ivory, and exotic animals with neighboring civilizations.

Society and Culture:

Ancient Egyptian society was hierarchical and stratified, with the pharaoh at the apex of the social pyramid, followed by nobles, priests, scribes, artisans, and farmers. Social status was largely determined by birth, occupation, and proximity to the pharaoh. Family life was central to Egyptian society, with kinship ties and filial piety forming the basis of social cohesion. Art, literature, architecture, and science flourished in Ancient Egypt, with monumental achievements such as the construction of the pyramids, the development of hieroglyphic writing, and advancements in medicine, mathematics, and astronomy.

Religion and Beliefs:

Religion held a central place in Ancient Egyptian society, permeating every aspect of life. The Egyptians worshipped a pantheon of gods and goddesses who were believed to control the forces of nature and the cosmos. The pharaoh served as the intermediary between the gods and the people, responsible for maintaining cosmic order and ensuring the prosperity of the kingdom. Religious rituals, ceremonies, and festivals were conducted to honor the gods, venerate the ancestors, and appease malevolent spirits.

Decline and Legacy:

The decline of the Egyptian Empire began in the Late Period, marked by internal strife, foreign invasions, and the loss of political unity. The conquest of Egypt by Alexander the Great in 332 BCE and subsequent rule by the Ptolemaic dynasty heralded the beginning of Greek influence in Egypt. The Roman conquest of Egypt in 30 BCE further transformed the region, leading to the decline of traditional Egyptian culture and the rise of Christianity as the dominant religion.

Despite its political decline, the legacy of Ancient Egypt endures as one of the greatest civilizations in history. Egypt's contributions to art, architecture, literature, science, and religion continue to inspire and captivate people around the world. The pyramids, temples, and tombs of Egypt stand as testaments to the ingenuity and creativity of the ancient Egyptians, while their language, writing system, and religious beliefs continue to fascinate scholars and enthusiasts alike. Egypt remains a symbol of resilience, innovation, and cultural heritage, a timeless reminder of the enduring power of human civilization.

www.ingramcontent.com/pod-product-compliance
Lightning Source LLC
Chambersburg PA
CBHW060915140726
47996CB00001B/252